INSIGHTS *into* BUSINESS

INSIGHTS *into* BUSINESS

MICHAEL LANNON

GRAHAM TULLIS

TONYA TRAPPE

 LONGMAN

Addison Wesley Longman Limited
Edinburgh Gate, Harlow,
Essex CM20 2JE, England
and Associated Companies
throughout the world.

This edition published by Addison Wesley
Longman 1996
Sixth impression 1997

ISBN 0-17-555989-9

Produced by Longman Asia Limited, Hong Kong,
SWTC/06

Acknowledgements

The authors would like to thank the
following for their help: Ben Marsh, Linda
Kehr Grams, Jill A Berke, 3M plc, St Paul
MN; Pip Frankish 3M UK plc and Hervé
Naux of 3M France; Peter Iwarson, MoDo;
Gerald Adams, Utah State University;
Joanna Lawrence, ICI; Nathalie Baudoin,
Patagonia GMBH; Norman A. Jacobs,
Eastpak, Inc.; Meda Stamper, The Coca
Cola Company; John L. Henry, Uniglobe
Travel (International) Inc.; American
Management Association, New York; Polly
Platt; Intercultural Management Associates;
Business Principles London; Ancient
Recipes; Dan Cassidy, Glasgow
Polytechnic; Association of British Insurers;
David Brodala, Perfect Pizza; The City
Business Library, London; INSEAD
Library, Fontainbleau, France; Peter J.
Griffiths, Reuters, London; International
Management, The Manager and Staff of the
Longacre Body Shop, London; Phil Talbot,
Pascale du Verne and Tracey Pearce of The
Body Shop; Rhys Davis of Business; James
Johnson-Flint, Richer Sounds plc; Dr Leigh
Sparks, Stirling University Institute for
Retail Studies; Maureen Cork, Banking
Information Service, London; Caroline
Paylor, Colin Mayes, London Stock
Exchange; Anne Blisset, Jeanette Newman,
Ivor Googe, Corporate Communications,
BP plc, British Franchising Association;
Renault, France Ltd.

The publishers would like to thank the
following for their kind permission to use
their material in this book:

Eurobusiness for 3M: An American Star in
Europe by Tim Hindle, p.6; Colgate
Palmolive, p.9; MoDo, p.12; Virgin France,
p.146; *International Herald Tribune*, Looks:
Appearance Counts With Many Managers
by Sherry Buchanan, p.16; Patagonia
GMBH, Munich, p.18; Renault UK Ltd,
p.21; *The European*, Be nice and smile if
you want to hire a Hungarian manager,
Steve Lodge; *The Washington Post*, In Ads,
US Stars Shine For Japanese Eyes Only by
Margaret Shapiro, p.36; The Coca-Cola
Company, Atlanta, p.39; *The European*,
Small Slice of the Big Action by Iain
McKilvie, p.45; Benetton Public Relations,
France, p.48; Uniglobe Travel
(International) Inc., p.47; Perfect Pizza, UK,
p.51; Budget Rent a Car International Inc.,
UK, p.51-2, 148; *US News and World
Report*, Dying to Work by Jim Impoco, p.54;
Cartoonists and Writers Syndicate, p.61;
World Press Review, p.61; *Inc.*, A Banner of
Values, by Bo Burlingham, p.63; The Body
Shop, p.51-68; The Proctor and Gamble
Company, p.67; *Business*, Richer Pickings
by Nigel Cope, p.71; Richer Sounds plc,
p.73; Marks and Spencer, p.73; Bank of
Scotland, Hobs, p.80; Lombard Bank, p.150;
Banking Information Service, London, The
Stock Exchange, p.90; *The Independent*,
p.94, 152; Thorntons p.92; *Time*, Getting
together by Michael S. Serrill, p.99;
Motokov, p.101; Renault, p.147; *Financial
Times*, Deliver us from debt by Nicholas
Garnett, p.108; *Super Marketing*, The
Spanish Oracle by Keely Harrison, p.118;
British Invisibles Corporation of London,
Insurance Services p.129; Prudential
Corporation plc., London, p.132; BP plc,
p.137, 139; Perrier p.141.

The authors would also like to thank the
following people for their co-operation in
allowing us to interview them: Manley
Johnson, 3M France, p.10, 11; David Smyth,
Europe Assistance, p.22; Tom Scheck,
Profile. p.31; Manfred Kozlowsky, Harley-
Davidson GMH, p.41; John P. Hayes, The
Hayes Group Inc., p.50; Kay Ainsley,
Domino's Pizza, p.50; Klaus G. Ueber,
Natural Beauty Products Ltd, p.50; Tony
Dutfield, British Franchise Association,
p.44; Tomomi Moriwake, p.59; David
Wheeler, Body Shop, p.68; Dr Steve Burt,
Stirling University Institute for Retail
Studies, p.70; Peter Milson, Midland Bank,
p.78; Alain Depussé, p.86; Stuart Valentine,
The London Stock Exchange, p.97;
Margareta Galfard, Volvo, France, p.105;
Ben Fox, Fasta Pasta, p.107, 113; OECD,
Paris, p.116, 127; Glen Tuttsell, Michael
Peters Ltd, p.142.

Photographs

ATS, p.142; The Bank of Scotland, p.80;
British Broadcasting Corporation, p.142;
Benetton Public Relations, France, p.48;
BMW, p.103; The Body Shop International
plc, p.62-5, 68; Stuart Boreham
Photography, p.18; BP plc, p.137, 139-41;
Budget Rent a Car, p.52; J. Allan Cash
Photo Library, p.77; The Coca Cola
Company, p.34; Eastpak Inc., p.40; Fiat,
p.104; The Financial Times/ Tony Andrews,
p.108; Harley-Davidson, p.41; Harrods Ltd,
p.69; IBM, p.34; Kentucky Fried Chicken,
p.43; Kwik Fit, p.43; Lexus Cars, p.104;
Mars Confectionery, p.34; The Midland
Bank, p.78; Modo, p.12; The Image Bank,
p.32; Perfect Pizza, p.51; Perrier, p.141;
Philips, p.31; Reed Business Publications,
p.118; Keith Reed, p.19, 45, 69, 71, 111;
Renault Cars, p.104-105; Rex Features p.36,
99, 130; Chris Ridgers Photography, p.9, 34,
77; Marcus Robinson, p.129; The Science
Photo Library p.67; The Telegraph Colour
Library, p.117; Tesco Creative Services,
p.69; Thorntons Confectionery, p.92; Tony
Stone Worldwide, p.11, 16, 54, 56, 77, 78;
3M, p.5-8; Vauxhall Cars, p.112; Walkers
Shortbread Ltd, p.40.

Illustrated by Helen E. Porter.

Contents

Introduction

Insights into Business is intended as an intermediate to upper-intermediate Business English course both for students of business and practising business people. It provides students with an authentic framework in which to develop their understanding of key areas of contemporary business, while at the same time giving them the opportunity to improve their language skills through a wide variety of relevant and challenging activities.

The material contained in *Insights into Business* has been selected in order to meet the curriculum and syllabus requirements of a Business Studies course and is therefore ideal for students preparing for these examinations. At the same time considerable emphasis has been placed on the development of students' communicative skills through the interactive group or pair work activities that are an integral part of each unit.

One of the priorities throughout the research and writing of this course has been to ensure that current business practices have been reflected as realistically as possible. To achieve this the authors have worked in close collaboration with a number of major companies and institutions. This has made it possible to present the different topics in a more vivid and appealing way, which is particularly relevant to today's students.

In short, *Insights into Business* is an enjoyable and stimulating course which will help students acquire the necessary skills to operate effectively in an English-speaking professional environment.

Each unit of the book is structured as follows:

KEY VOCABULARY

This short introductory section familiarises students with the theme of the unit and provides explanations of the core vocabulary. Key words are shown in bold and either given with corresponding definitions or presented in such a way that their meanings can easily be deduced from the context.

The theme of the unit can be presented orally and students asked to contribute any relevant vocabulary that they may already have. At this stage attention should be drawn to the words highlighted in the Key Vocabulary section by, for example, writing them on the board. Alternatively, and particularly for larger groups, students may be asked to study this section beforehand. Students' comprehension of these key words should be checked before going further into the unit.

LEAD-IN

The Lead-in section is intended to generate interest in the unit topic. It takes various forms, from a listening exercise to a speaking activity that involves either pair work or discussion, and encourages students to reflect on the subject-matter. It also invites them to contribute any relevant personal experience or knowledge that they may already have. More details on how to exploit this material will be found in each unit.

READING

Each unit includes a reading passage taken from a British or American newspaper, business publication or company literature. While some of these texts provide an overview of the subject of the unit, others have been chosen because they present from an individual perspective the people or issues involved. The passages, which vary in length and degree of difficulty, may be read either in class or prepared beforehand. Comprehension can then be checked in the exercises that follow, which include activities such as true/false, multiple-choice and grid completion.

VOCABULARY

Each reading passage is followed by two or three vocabulary exercises. The first one or two test students' comprehension of topic-related vocabulary items taken from the passage through a variety of tasks. These include matching definitions, finding synonyms or antonyms, word building and crossword puzzles. The final exercise activates this vocabulary by providing a different context in which students can demonstrate that they are able to use the new words. Use of an English-English dictionary is encouraged whenever necessary.

DISCUSSION

The Discussion section allows the class as a whole to express ideas and opinions related to the theme of the reading passage. In some units a series of general questions is provided as a stimulus, while in others students are asked to comment on documents, information or case studies which are provided as additional input.

LANGUAGE FOCUS

The book contains a standard syllabus of grammatical structures that students at intermediate and upper-intermediate level should in theory have already mastered but which in practice often need to be revised. The Language Focus section tackles one or more such structures and encourages students to consider the grammar in question and how it operates; and it includes a Practice section which allows students to consolidate their knowledge. Comprehensive explanations of these structures are given in the Grammar Reference section at the back of the book. In some units additional exercises are provided in order to focus on certain problem areas of grammar which appear in the reading passage.

All grammar exercises and examples are based on factual information taken from a variety of original sources and will therefore enhance the students' knowledge of the general topic of the unit. The grammar exercises lend themselves well to use as homework assignments which can then be corrected in class.

SKILLS FOCUS

In order to develop the four skills each unit contains a series of activities which set practical tasks and encourage students to provide creative solutions to authentic business problems. This section enables students to consolidate and apply the knowledge they have acquired throughout the unit. In keeping with the overall philosophy of *Insights into Business*, these activities usually incorporate authentic materials provided by professional organisations. Full instructions on the organisation and timing of these activities can be found under the relevant headings in each unit of this book.

READING

The reading material in this section includes fact files, case studies, promotional materials and questionnaires. These documents require detailed study as students will need to refer to them and exploit their content during the subsequent stages of the activity. When a document contains a potential problem area, a full explanation is provided.

WRITING

The tasks presented in this section are mainly designed to introduce students to the most common forms of business correspondence (memos, letters of request and complaint, letters of application, reports etc.). Students are also given the chance to express their personal views in other types of writing assignments.

LISTENING

In addition to the listening passages which sometimes form part of a Lead-in, each unit includes a separate Listening section in which students will hear extracts from interviews with representatives of companies or specialists in each of the fifteen areas of business covered in the book. Students thus have direct contact with people who provide valuable insights based on their personal experience and first-hand knowledge. The listening tasks have been devised mainly to draw attention to these ideas, rather than systematically exploiting their grammatical and lexical content.

It should be noted that the interviews are authentic and were recorded with both native and non-native speakers of English; they therefore contain the hesitations, rephrasing and unconventional syntax which are a feature of natural speech. Instructions on how to use the listening materials, along with the tapescripts, appear in the relevant sections in this book.

SPEAKING

Proficiency in spoken English is developed through different and often interrelated stages which combine role play and discussion in small groups. The objective of the role play activities is to prepare students to function in situations where they will need to use specific skills such as interviewing, making and replying to enquiries, asking for and giving advice, etc. Suggested expressions are provided where appropriate. The small group discussion work, however, concentrates on providing students with a context in which they can express their own ideas and comments more freely. Very often a final speaking activity allows the class as a whole to compare and evaluate the work that was done in small groups or pairs.

Map of Students' Book

	PRE-READING	TEXT	LANGUAGE FOCUS	SKILLS FOCUS
UNIT 1 **COMPANY STRUCTURES**	Listening – The departments of an organisation 3M Corporate Organisation Chart	READING – '3M: An American Star in Europe' *(Eurobusiness)*	Present perfect and Past simple Describing changes in quantities (increase and decrease)	LISTENING – Describing responsibilities within a company: Manley Johnson, 3M France SPEAKING – Presenting companies WRITING – Company profiles
UNIT 2 **RECRUITMENT**	Matching job advertisements with covering letters	READING – 'Looks: appearance counts with many managers' *(International Herald Tribune)*	Present simple and Present continuous	READING – Studying job advertisements WRITING – Preparing a CV and letter of application LISTENING – Selecting candidates and job interviews – David Smyth, Europe Assistance SPEAKING – Role play of an interview
UNIT 3 **MANAGEMENT STYLES**	Management styles in five different countries	READING – 'Be nice and smile if you want to hire a Hungarian manager' *(The European)*	Adjectives of nationality Expressing fractions and proportions	LISTENING – Tom Scheck talks about the problems involved in international negotiations SPEAKING – Cultural differences – Role play: Giving and asking for advice
UNIT 4 **ADVERTISING AND MARKETING**	Advertising media Product endorsements Advertising slogans	READING – 'In Ads, US Stars Shine For Japanese Eyes Only' *(Washington Post)*	Gerund and Infinitive	SPEAKING – Describing target markets; Analysing advertisements LISTENING – Customer profiles and marketing strategy: Manfred Kozlowsky, Harley-Davidson
UNIT 5 **FRANCHISING**	Categories of franchises Listening – Tony Dutfield of the British Franchise Association	READING – 'Small slice of the Big Action' *(The European)*	Relative clauses	LISTENING – Three executives discuss franchisor/franchisee relations – Interview with Peter Stern, senior franchise manager for the National Westminster Bank SPEAKING – Taking out a franchise with Budget Rent a Car and Perfect Pizza WRITING – Report on UK franchise market
UNIT 6 **JAPAN AND THE BUSINESS WORLD**	The performance of Japanese business Comparison of hours worked in different countries	READING – 'Dying to work' *(US News and World Report)*	Expressing contrast	WRITING – The memo LISTENING – Tips for doing business in Japan: Tomomi Moriwake
UNIT 7 **BUSINESS AND THE ENVIRONMENT**	Environmental cartoons The role of business in environmental affairs	READING – 'A banner of values' *(Inc.)*	The Passive Describing groups and subgroups	SPEAKING – Environmental case studies; Labels and packaging LISTENING – A Body Shop customer survey; The role of companies and environmental affairs: David Wheeler, The Body Shop WRITING – Are your purchasing decisions based on environmental concerns?

	PRE-READING	TEXT	LANGUAGE FOCUS	SKILLS FOCUS
UNIT 8 **RETAILING**	Retailing in the UK and in continental Europe Listening – Dr Steve Burt, Stirling University	READING – 'Richer pickings' *(Business)*	Make or do Locating objects	LISTENING – Store layouts SPEAKING/WRITING – Consumer buying habits
UNIT 9 **BANKING**	Listening – Peter Milson, Midland Bank Banking items and documents	READING – 'Hobs' Home and Office Banking System *(Bank of Scotland brochure)*	Allow/enable/let First and second conditional	SPEAKING – Making and answering enquiries about bank documents LISTENING – Alain Depussé, French businessman: a company and its banks WRITING – A letter of complaint to a bank
UNIT 10 **THE STOCK EXCHANGE**	Headlines from the financial pages – Assessing the performance of listed companies' shares	READING – 'The Stock Exchange' *(Banking Information Service)*	Third conditional	READING – Studying share price listings LISTENING – European stock market turnovers. Characteristics of stock exchanges: Stuart Valentine of the London Stock Exchange WRITING – Summarising the evolution of a company's share prices
UNIT 11 **CORPORATE ALLIANCES AND ACQUISITIONS**	Extracts from the financial press	READING – 'Getting Together' *(Time)*	Reported speech	SPEAKING – Describing technical data and performance of cars LISTENING – The Renault/Volvo alliance – Margareta Galfard, Volvo, France WRITING – Memo recommending a course of action
UNIT 12 **THE SMALL BUSINESS**	Advantages and disadvantages of small business Listening – Checklist for starting a business: Ben Fox of Fasta Pasta	READING – 'Deliver us from debt' *(Financial Times)*	Could have + past participle Should have + past participle	LISTENING – Advice for starting a business: Ben Fox, Fasta Pasta SPEAKING – Small business questionnaire WRITING – Business plan
UNIT 13 **INTERNATIONAL TRADE**	Listening – Why countries trade OECD Economist Europe quiz	READING – 'A Spanish Oracle' *(Super Marketing)*	Modal verbs of obligation Describing trends	WRITING – Describing the evolution of wool prices from a graph LISTENING – An economist from the OECD speaks about protectionism and the European Community's Common Agricultural Policy SPEAKING – Completing a graph
UNIT 14 **INSURANCE**	Listening – Identifying types of risk	READING – 'Insurance Services' *(Corporation of London brochure)*	Expressing approximation	LISTENING – Don Raley, insurance expert, talks about Lloyds SPEAKING – Evaluating risk WRITING – Report on evaluation of risk forms
UNIT 15 **CORPORATE IDENTITY**	Analysing a BP corporate advertisement	READING – 'How the decisions were made' *(An Image for the 90s – from a BP publication)*	The Article	LISTENING – Glen Tuttsel of the Michael Peters' design consultancy talks about logos, design and corporate identity SPEAKING – Convincing a sponsor WRITING – Request letter

Company Structures

KEY VOCABULARY

Introduce the topic by asking students to present a typical company structure, writing their ideas on the board in the form of a chart. This will help students to visualise the structure of a company. Have students read through the vocabulary section in the unit and introduce the organisation chart, presenting the hierarchy from top to bottom, asking students to comment on how it compares to their own diagram. Ensure that students have understood the meaning of the words in bold before they continue further with the unit.

LEAD-IN

1 The purpose of this task is to show students some of the different responsibilities that employees have within the departments which have just been studied. Play the tape as many times as is necessary for the students to extract the required information. Students should compare answers after they have listened to all six extracts. At this point you may wish to play the extracts which caused particular difficulty again, pointing out some of the vocabulary which might be unfamiliar to the students such as report, accountants (speaker 1) and design (speaker 2).

Key:

1 Finance
2 Research and Development
3 Marketing
4 Public Relations
5 Production
6 Personnel (or Human Resources)

Tapescript:

SPEAKER 1: Every six months we produce a report showing how the company is doing. This past week, we've been busy with our accountants preparing the results that will be included in our next report.

SPEAKER 2: I'm a member of a team of engineers and we've just finalised the design of our new portable computer. This model will be more powerful and more adaptable than our previous one. We're constantly looking for new ideas and experimenting with new products.

SPEAKER 3: Before selling our latest product, our department must decide in which regions it will be the most successful and what types of consumer we want to reach.

SPEAKER 4: Communication is a key aspect of my department's work. We answer enquiries made by our customers and are also in contact with the press to inform them of new products and changes within the company.

SPEAKER 5: We've been having problems with the quality of certain electronic parts made in our factories. So several members of the department have got together to talk about ways of improving some of our manufacturing techniques.

SPEAKER 6: Our company is going through a difficult period and we have had to reduce the number of employees in several departments and to review salaries throughout the organisation.

2 This task is a continuation of the previous one and is based on the company which will be featured in the unit, 3M. Working in pairs or small groups, students refer to the 3M Corporate Organisation chart in order to decide which department or sector is responsible for each of the items 1–7. Go round to each group, checking that they have understood the more difficult vocabulary.

Key:

1 Life Sciences Sector
2 Information, Imaging and Electronic Sector
3 Life Sciences Sector
4 Human Resources
5 Industrial and Consumer Sector
6 International Operations
7 Information, Imaging and Electronic Sector

READING

1 Encourage students to read the article as quickly as possible, focussing on comprehension questions 1–4. At this stage they should not worry unduly about unknown vocabulary.

Note: Corundum is a hard mineral often used as an abrasive of which ruby and sapphire are varieties.

Key:

1 The company's full name is Minnesota Mining and Manufacturing. At the beginning of the century the company was involved in mining but this activity stopped shortly after.
2 3M is successful due to its strong commitment to technological innovation. It invests heavily in research and development of new products.
3 The EMATS are responsible for achieving 3M's European goals. They meet regularly to discuss the launch of new products.
4 3M must learn to adapt to change and to come up with products to meet the demands of its European customers.

2 This exercise provides an opportunity to do some work on numbers, often a problem area in English. Once students have found the answers to the comprehension exercise, they should practise reading the figures aloud in pairs, before listening to the cassette to check their pronunciation. It may be useful at this stage to remind students that in English we do not make the words *hundred*, *thousand* or *million* plural when in a large number, for example: we never say *£4 millions* but £4 million. Also with decimals we say 4.32 as *four point three two* not *four comma thirty two*.

Point out equally that in English *and* separates the hundreds and the numbers which follow:

12,839 =	*twelve thousand eight hundred and thirty-nine*
452,210 =	*four hundred and fifty-two thousand two hundred and ten*
6,391,000 =	*six million three hundred and ninety-one thousand*

'And' is also used in numbers which contain no hundreds:

| 2,021 = | *two thousand and twenty one.* |

Key:

1	$200 million	4	15	7	150
2	17	5	36%	8	30%
3	14	6	6.5%		

3 Play the tape through with short pauses for the students to write down the numbers.

Tapescript and key:

1	7.4%	4	1,001	7	£6,391,152
2	364	5	13.57	8	0.2%
3	12,839	6	$451,210		

VOCABULARY

1 Encourage students to look at the words in context in order to deduce their meanings.

Key:

1	c	4	h	7	b
2	e	5	a	8	d
3	g	6	f		

2 The students should scan the text in order to find words with the same meaning as those in bold in the sentences.

Key:

1	subsidiaries	6	headquarters
2	in charge of; set up	7	achieving; goals
3	sectors	8	launch
4	run; staff	9	come up with
5	strategy		

3 The purpose of this exercise is to activate some of the vocabulary that students have studied in Exercises 1 and 2.

Key:

1	innovate	6	research
2	launch	7	strategy
3	patent	8	headquarters
4	performance	9	staff
5	budget	10	come up with

DISCUSSION

Free discussion questions.

LANGUAGE FOCUS

Present Perfect and Past Simple

Focus students attention on the sentences from the text and use the questions to form the basis of a class discussion on the differences between the present perfect and past simple tenses. If you wish, students can refer to the Grammar Reference section, page 153.

Practice

Before reading the article and completing the exercise, ask students what they know about Colgate Palmolive. How many products can they name which are manufactured by the company?

Key:

1	founded	7	has increased	13	has maintained
2	did	8	have grown	14	has enlarged
3	began	9	exceeded	15	has been
4	led	10	has developed	16	has always paid
5	has set up	11	bought	17	has already made
6	has become	12	has had	18	chose

Describing Changes

Practice

Key:

1 decrease/reduce
2 increased/rose/went up
3 decreased/fallen/gone down/declined
4 decrease/fall/decline
5 increase/rise
6 decrease/fall/drop/decline

SKILLS FOCUS

LISTENING

1 Before listening to the cassette, the students should study the structures while referring back to the 3M organisation chart at the beginning of the unit. Try asking additional questions based on the chart to make sure that the students use the structures properly (in particular *responsible for*, not *responsible of*). Students already in employment could be asked to describe their responsibilities and positions in their present jobs or in jobs that they might have had in the past. Remind students that articles are always used in English before jobs for example: *He is a journalist. I am the Marketing Manager of 3M.* and point out that the gerund form is used after prepositions for example: *in charge of doing something, responsible for doing something.*

2 The purpose of this activity is to have students listen for the information missing from the table. The more technical words such as non-slip or abrasive can be explained beforehand.

Key:

Division or sector	Number of years spent in position	Name of superior	Responsibilities
Building Service and Cleaning Products	–	–	*Worked on improving many products including non-slip materials*
Industrial Laboratories	–	*Ron Mitch*	*Developed Scotch Guard*
Industrial Scotch-brite products	*4 years*	*Dr Chuck Rich*	*Managed the technical aspects of the business*
Life Sciences	*3½ years*	–	*Identified important technologies and strategies for the company's future business*
Disposable Products	*3 years*	–	*Worked with the technical staffs of major customers to identify their needs*

Tapescript:

Mr Manley Johnson began working for 3M in 1968 after completing his studies in organic chemistry at the University of Illinois. He first joined the Building Service and Cleaning Products Division where he worked on improving many different products, including non-slip materials, used on stairs and in bathtubs.

He also worked as a supervisor in the Industrial Laboratories Division and worked under a man called Ron Mitsch. He developed 'Scotch Guard', which is used to protect carpets and is now sold throughout the world.

Mr Johnson then took on responsibilities in the Industrial Scotch-Brite Sector which manufactures and sells abrasive and cleaning products. He was in charge of managing the technical aspects of this business for four years and reported to Dr Chuck Rich.

He spent the next three and a half years as Technical Director of the Life Sciences Sector. He was responsible for identifying important technologies for the company's future business and worked with various divisions to find the right strategies for developing these technologies.

A position which Mr Johnson held for three years was that of Technical Director of the Disposable Products Division. He worked very closely with the technical staffs of major customers to identify their specific needs. He found this to be a very interesting and exciting job.

3 The first time the students listen to the tape, they should be listening for global comprehension and the second time for specific details which should be written down in note form. Check the descriptions written by the students to make sure that the important information has not been overlooked.

Key:

Suggested description of Mr Johnson's job:

Manley Johnson is the Technical Director of 3M France, which includes direct responsibility for 15 European laboratories. He makes decisions concerning technical partnerships and patents and is responsible for finding the right people to work in the company. He believes that an important part of his job is making sure that his technical staff have strong careers and opportunities because they will run the company in the future.

Mr Johnson's position is equivalent to that of H A Hammerly Executive Vice President International Operations.

Tapescript:

My job is really the Technical Director of France and it includes having direct responsibility for our European laboratories (the laboratories I've just described) and we have responsibility for about 15 divisions across Europe. We have some 90 people directly involved in those efforts.

So I view, a very important part of my job is to bring the 3M R & D culture here, to make sure that people talk to each other, they share technologies, they understand what's going on within the technical community, that there is good career plans and good personnel decisions made within the technical community, even though the people might not work directly in my organisation, I think that's one of my roles.

I think another very important part of my responsibilities overall is to be the technical officer of 3M France, to make sure that when we enter into agreements, we do so carefully and logically and we identify good technical partnerships, make sure that our patents are well done and we patent the right things so that I have a responsibility for the intellectual property as well. And I think, as I mentioned earlier, a large part is the human resource aspect, to make sure that our technical people have strong careers and opportunities, because, one of my most important jobs, I think, is to hire the right people, and there's a tremendous talent pool here in France that we have to access if we're going to compete globally. So, we have to make sure that we hire the best and give them the best opportunities because they're the people that will be running the company some day.

SPEAKING

1 This short role play activity is designed to reinforce the students' command of the structures studied in the pre-listening section. At the same time, it will enable them to review the questions that are usually asked when introducing oneself during first meetings. As the students prepare their list of questions, make sure that a wide variety of structures are being thought of in order to obtain information, such as *How old are you?*, *How much money do you earn?*, *What kind of company do you work for?*, and *Where did you study?* instead of *What is your age?*, *What is your salary?*, *What is your company?*, *What is your background*, etc.

The correctness of the structures used can also be monitored by listening to each group during the interview stage.

Recruitment

2 Each student should spend about ten minutes reading the profile of their company and should then ask their partner for the information needed in order to fill in the chart. As the students work in pairs, make sure that they ask each other questions and exchange information rather than simply re-read the profiles. It may be useful to introduce additional structures that can be used to ask for the information in the chart: *Where is the company based?* in addition to *Where are the company's headquarters?*; *How many people does the company employ?* in addition to *How many people work for the company?*, etc.

Key:

Name of Company	MoDo	Virgin
Headquarters	Stockholm	London
Chairman	Bernt Lof	Richard Branson
Business Activities	fine paper, newsprint and magazine paper, other wood products	music, entertainment, communications and travel
Main Markets	Europe and the USA	USA, Canada, Australia, Japan
Sales in 1990	18.4 million kronor*	£1100 million (1991)
Number of Employees	About 12,961	Over 6,000

* It may be worth mentioning that the Swedish currency is the Krona (plural Kronor) and not to be confused with the Krone (plural Kroner), the standard monetary unit of Norway and Denmark.

WRITING

This activity can be either done in class, in pairs or small groups, or used as an individual homework assignment.

Suggested answer:

The headquarters of ICI (Imperial Chemical Industries) are in London. Its main areas of business are industrial chemicals, materials, pharmaceutical products, paints and agrochemicals. The industrial chemicals sector accounted for** 24% of the company's total sales in 1991. The company sells its products in over 150 countries and can be found in 600 different locations. In 1991, the ICI Group employed over 128,000 people throughout the world, of which 51,600 were employed in the UK.

**Draw attention to the structure *to account for* which also appears in the text (line 40): *Europe accounts for some 30% of the company's worldwide sales and one quarter of its employees.*

KEY VOCABULARY

Read through the key vocabulary with the students and illustrate the 'appointments page' by bringing to class the relevant pages from newspapers and magazines, pointing out the other titles that are sometimes used such as *job offers*, *situations vacant* etc. You may also want to draw attention to the derivatives: *to apply – application – applicant – application form, to recruit – recruitment*; and to the fact that at an interview there is an *interviewer* and an *interviewee*.

LEAD-IN

1 This activity may be done in pairs or small groups. Check that the students understand the vocabulary used in the job advertisements and application letter extracts; for example, words like *chartered accountants, university degree, non-contributory pension, relocation* and *word-processing skills* may need explanation. Once the exercise has been completed, encourage the students to discuss the jobs and say which, if any, would appeal to them.

Students should not worry too much about specific details in the advertisements. They should be reading for global sense and for certain key words which will allow them to complete the exercise.

Key:

1	d	3	e	5	c
2	a	4	b		

2 This exercise is designed to reinforce important vocabulary relating to the topic under study. Check that the students have fully understood the vocabulary and that they are not simply copying down the relevant part of the advertisements.

Key:

Requirements	Benefits
1 – IPM qualification – Minimum of 3 years' experience – Educated to degree level	– Competitive salary – Non-contributory pension – 25 days' holiday – Private health insurance – Relocation assistance
2 – Advanced degree in business administration or similar – 5 years' international office management experience	– Competitive international salary – Overseas allowance

- Fluency in French and English
- Must be prepared to travel, live and work in difficult conditions

3 – Qualification in Engineering
  – Several years' experience in computer assisted technology
  – Excellent salary
  – Sales-related bonus
  – Company car

4 – Science degree
  – Subsidised staff canteen

5 – Efficiency
  – Good administrative and secretarial abilities
  – Salary dependent on age and experience

3 These statements have been selected for their sometimes provocative content and should therefore lead to a lively debate. Emphasis should not, at this stage, be placed on accuracy, but on expression of ideas. You may need to explain the word *morphopsychology* which is featured in the subsequent reading text on 'Looks'.

READING

This text is taken from the International Herald Tribune and includes American spellings of words such as *colour* (Am. Eng. color) and *metre* (Am. Eng. meter).

Key:

1	T	3	T	5	F
2	F	4	T		

DISCUSSION

These discussion questions differ from the statements in the lead-in section, in so far as they are based more on the text than on the theme in general. Students are also encouraged to think about some of the questions raised in the text as well as about recruitment practices in their own country.

VOCABULARY

1 Encourage students to look at the words in context in order to deduce their meaning.

Key:

1	f	6	d
2	g	7	i
3	j	8	c
4	a	9	e
5	b	10	h

2 It may be useful to give a brief explanation of the term *headhunter* as students may not be aware of the expression in English.

Key:

1	hire	4	career
2	qualities	5	employer
3	requires	6	applicants

LANGUAGE FOCUS

PRESENT SIMPLE AND PRESENT CONTINUOUS

This exercise reviews the different uses of the present simple and present continuous and is designed to check the students' awareness of the function and usage of these tenses.

Key:

1	c	3	b	5	g	7	e
2	f	4	d	6	a		

Practice

Key:

1	wants	9	says
2	feels	10	decide
3	is not using	11	travels
4	is looking for	12	enjoys
5	realises	13	is attending
6	is growing	14	is going
7	reads	15	suggest
8	is living		

SKILLS FOCUS

Reading

This activity presents the students with an unusual job advertisement to study in detail. Certain words may have to be explained e.g: *mother tongue, glamor*, (Br. Eng. glamour) and *gritty*.

Key:

1 Nathalie Baudoin
2 Public affairs associate
3 Sportswear
4 PR/Press experience, good writing skills, proficiency in technical sports and German mother tongue
5 Munich
6 California

Preparation for writing

1 The curriculum vitae

This activity offers the students an opportunity to study the layout and content of the curriculum vitae in English. It will also serve as a model for future reference.

Key:

1 PERSONAL DETAILS
2 EDUCATION
3 PROFESSIONAL EXPERIENCE
4 INTERESTS
5 ADDITIONAL SKILLS
6 REFERENCES

The students are asked to look at the order of the dates and say what they notice about them. This is to draw their attention to the fact that in English, the dates on a CV are very often given in reverse order. There are many other ways of organising a CV; discuss the various possibilities with the students and ask them to select their own preference.

2 The letter of application

This activity invites students to study the vocabulary and the information contained in a standard covering letter. As well as being a useful model for their personal future reference, it will also help students to complete the writing activity which follows.

Key:

1	apply	**6**	matches
2	advertised	**7**	involved
3	employed	**8**	enjoy
4	welcome	**9**	discuss
5	notice	**10**	contact

3 Free discussion activity.

WRITING

This activity provides students with an opportunity to practise writing their own letters of application and curricula vitae. Read the advertisement with the students checking that they have fully understood what is required by Renault. The students can then invent a CV and letter of application which correspond to the requirements mentioned in the advertisement. This can be done in groups or given as a homework assignment. In either case it would be useful to collect the work and correct it outside class. In this way part of the following class can be devoted to pointing out some of the mistakes made by the students and how these can be rectified.

LISTENING

1 Play the cassette once to allow the students to complete the first exercise.

Key:

b the qualities a candidate must have
d the kind of things a candidate is expected to know
a the mistakes a candidate can make at an interview
c his advice to interviewees

Play the extract a second time for students to find the specific information required.

Explain what is meant by *notes* and point out that this exercise is not designed to be a dictation.

Key:

b An ability to react quickly, be intelligent, be suitable for the position. The person should be well presented, be nice and tidy.

d He should have a knowledge of what the company does, what he is going to be expected to do, who he is going to report to.

a To say *yes* to everything.

c Listen, ask the right questions, create a good relationship with the interviewer.

Tapescript:

PERSONNEL MANAGER: The most important thing when interviewing a candidate is his character, his ability to react, his intelligence and his suitability for the position that which, for which he is being interviewed.

QUESTION: And uh, to what extent does the person's appearance influence your decision?

PERSONNEL MANAGER: It doesn't influence the decision, uh, but it does have some bearing on the decision, if you can take the difference between the two. It is important that the guy, the person, is well presented, is neat and tidy, and that he has a good manner, uh because that shows a lot about his personality.

QUESTION: Do you expect the candidate to be prepared in any way for the interview, or how should he prepare himself for the interview?

PERSONNEL MANAGER: Well, it's not a question of preparing himself. In the position in which I am, uh, normally the candidate's had at least one or maybe two interviews with other members, more junior members of staff before he gets to my level, unless the particular candidate is going to report directly to me, and in which case I expect the person concerned to have a fairly good knowledge of: (1) what the company does, (2) what he's going to be expected to do, and (3) who he's going to report to. Those things, those three items are very very important and if the candidate, uh, does not give an impression of either understanding one of those three items, then obviously then he gets marked down accordingly.

QUESTION: How does a candidate go wrong?

PERSONNEL MANAGER: The major way a candidate goes wrong is by basically becoming a yes-man or a yes-woman and agreeing with everything you say. What is most important … one of the most important things about interviewing a candidate is the chemistry between somebody, between the two people in that interview, em, it's very very important – he has to have a spark, you have to feel as though that guy is going to contribute, that guy's going to be good and you're going to get something out of that person and he has to show himself to be not just 'Yes sir, thank you very much. Yes I agree with that. I agree with that, I agree with that.' Sometimes I lay dummy questions, in which I want a 'no' answer and if he continues to say 'yes' then he goes down.

QUESTION: What would your advice be to a candidate, um, going to an interview. How would you advise him?

PERSONNEL MANAGER: Uh, the first thing I would say to him is first of all to listen, secondly, to ask the right questions, and thirdly, perhaps the most important, is to create the right kind of relationship which is, I guess is what you call an adult-to-adult relationship with the interviewee or the interviewer. It is very important and what I said before is when you get a yes-man in front of you, or a yes-woman, then that person is obviously not creating an adult-to-adult conversation, he's creating an adult-to-a-child conversation, and in most cases, managers are not, if they're good and they know what they want, they're not going to be interested in employing a child.

2

Key:

1 Interviewer is informed that the candidate has arrived.

2 Interviewer greets the candidate and brings him into the office.

3 Candidate is asked what he knows about the job and the company.

4 Interviewer reviews the CV.

5 Interviewer gives candidate his opinions on the job and the company.

6 Candidate asks questions for about 5 or 10 minutes.

7 Interviewer asks more general questions about the candidate's life, and adds one or two trick questions at the end of the interview.

Tapescript:

PERSONNEL MANAGER: The interview normally takes place by me being informed either by the secretary or the telephonist that the candidate has arrived, in which case, um, I leave my office and go and greet him in the reception area and bring him personally into my office and sit him down across the desk, or across my office desk to me, and we proceed, uh, from there . . . I normally start by asking the candidate to tell me what he . . . since he's been probably through two or three other interviews previous . . . what the job is that he's being expected to do, just to make sure that he understands fully.

Then I ask him to tell me a little bit about the company that we're working for, that I'm working for anyway, so that he's at least understood exactly what we do or the basics of what we do anyway . . . er then I normally review his CV, and in particular either his previous employment or current employment which is very important. Basically this is done to try and draw the candidate out, see how good he is at expressing himself, and to see what kind of character he is. Then I normally give him my view of what the position is that we're recruiting for and also my view about the company, then I normally give him a period of 5 or 10 minutes to ask some questions. Then I go back to him and just talk about him, and maybe then when he's fully relaxed, or more relaxed, put in a few of the trick questions, not a few, I would say usually normally one or maybe two maximum.

As I said in a previous question, it normally lasts a minimum of 45 minutes if the candidate is up to scratch and can go on for about an hour.

SPEAKING

This simulation exercise provides students with an opportunity to role play an actual interview situation thereby using the vocabulary seen throughout the unit. The activity involves both Student A and B in detailed preparation and therefore sufficient time should be allowed for this.

The A Students should use this time to decide how they will conduct the interview and what questions they will ask. As the students will be using the flow chart from the listening to help them, check that they have sufficiently prepared each stage of the interview i.e. well formulated questions relating to the CVs, information about the job and the company that they will give to the interviewee as well as more general or trick questions such as *What do you consider to be your strengths and weaknesses?* and *When did you last lose your temper?* The A Students should also try to anticipate the kinds of questions that The B Students will ask about the job and prepare their answers in advance.

The B Students should use the preparation time to review their CVs and to anticipate the questions that they will be asked relating to their education and work experience. They should also prepare questions to ask the interviewer about the job and the company.

During the actual interview the teacher should check that Student A is asking correctly formulated questions such as: *I see here that you worked during the summer holidays for XXXX. Could you tell me a little more about this?* and not questions like *What is your work experience?* and that Student B is not simply reading out his/her CV.

U N I T   3

Management Styles

KEY VOCABULARY

This section introduces the idea of the distribution of power in a business organisation and prepares the students for the exercise that follows. Check that the students have understood the key vocabulary shown in bold before they continue further with the unit.

LEAD-IN

1 This activity can be done in pairs or small groups. Using their general knowledge of the UK, USA, France, Germany and Sweden, the students should be able to identify which profile corresponds to each country. Lead into this exercise by asking what students feel to be the characteristics of each of these countries (i.e. by preparing a list of adjectives they associate with each national character).

Key:

1	Germany	4	United States
2	United Kingdom	5	France
3	Sweden		

2 Free discussion.

READING

	give and accept criticism	put profit above all else	make workers redundant	respond to financial incentives	judge staff on personal qualities rather than on their work	see their superiors outside of office hours
Hungary	–	✕	✕	✓	✓	✓
Bulgaria	–	–	–	✓	✕	✕
Poland	✓	–	✕	✓	✓	–
East Germany	–	✓	✓	✓	✕	–
West Germany	–	✕	–	–	–	✕
Spain	✕	–	–	–	–	✓
Italy	✕	–	–	–	–	✓
Greece	✕	–	–	–	✓	–

VOCABULARY

1 Key:

1	j	5	e	9	i
2	k	6	a	10	c
3	g	7	h	11	d
4	b	8	f		

Note: This may be a good opportunity to stress the difference between 'being made redundant' and 'being sacked'. The former is used when a person's job is no longer necessary, often because of economic reasons. 'Being sacked' or more formally 'being dismissed' implies a fault in the employee's work or conduct.

2 Key:

1	neighbour	5	manager
2	counterpart	6	recruit
3	westerner	7	supplier
4	worker	8	partner

3 This exercise reviews vocabulary previously studied in the text and tests students' understanding of it.

Key:

1	motivate	5	manager
2	meetings	6	profile
3	attitude	7	suit
4	relationship	8	rule

LANGUAGE FOCUS

ADJECTIVES OF NATIONALITY

Students may find that one or two of the companies are unknown to them in their country. Encourage them to find those with which they are familiar initially, moving on to those they are less sure about.

Key:

1. Philips is a Dutch electronics company.
2. Mateus Rosé is a Portuguese wine.
3. BBC 1 is a British television channel.
4. Ferrari is an Italian car manufacturer.
5. IBM is an American computer company.
6. AGFA is a German photographic company.
7. Cambio 16 is a Spanish weekly magazine.
8. Carlsberg is a Danish beer.
9. IKEA is a Swedish furniture retailer.
10. Evian is a French mineral water.
11. Olympic is a Greek airline.
12. Rolex is a Swiss watch.
13. Pravda is a Russian newspaper.
14. Aker AS is a Norwegian industrial company.
15. Istanbul is a Turkish seaport.
16. Neste is a Finnish chemical company.

Practice

1 Key:

1	three quarters	4	three out of five
2	more than half	5	nine out of ten
3	one in eight	6	a quarter

2 Key:

1	one out of ten	5	one third
2	half	6	three quarters
3	a quarter	7	three out of five
4	half		

SKILLS FOCUS

LISTENING

1 In the first listening extract the students are asked to listen for information in order to answer two questions. Play the cassette several times. During the first listening the students should listen for gist and the second time they should take notes. They should then use their notes to answer the questions. You may wish to point out that the speaker has a slight Czech accent.

Key:

1 They set up Profile because they saw a need for a better understanding between professionals from different cultural backgrounds, working in an international context.

2 They provide market information such as supply and demand, economic forecasts etc. as well as insights into the decision-making process in different cultural contexts.

2 Before listening to the second extract the students are asked to study the language of giving advice. Read through the passage with the students making sure that the structures in bold have been fully understood. Once this has been done the students can listen to the cassette for the specific information required. You may need to play the extract several times.

Key:

1 historical heritage
2 try to understand . . . on an international level
3 identical systems work differently
4 start negotiations with your local partner . . . business dealings
5 less efficient, less educated or less developed
6 flexible, open-minded and to listen
7 adapt your arguments

3 Before listening to the third extract ask the students to use their knowledge of the two countries in questions to try to guess what the speaker is going to say.

Key:

In France cars are presented in terms of:	In Holland cars are presented in terms of:
a Power	**a** Economy
b Technology	**b** Internal space and comfort

4 Before listening to the final extract the students should read the sentences and may, if they wish, try to answer the questions relying on their own knowledge. They could then check their answers while listening to the cassette.

Key:

1	F	4	T
2	T	5	T
3	F		

Tapescript:

1: We set up our company which is called Profile, a business consultancy in the international construction market, for different reasons.

First of all, all our associates are from different backgrounds and nationalities, all working in Paris, and we noticed that there is a need for a better understanding between professionals working in different contexts.

We provide more classical technical market information such as analysis of supply and demand, forecasts and economic assessments, as well as insights into the structure of decision-making in different contexts.

2: I'm going to talk about some basic problems we have encountered in our professional lives in the approach to international markets. It is important to remember first of all that every country has its own historical heritage and this defines the specific context, and you should always try to understand this context when doing business on an international level. Don't forget that identical systems work differently in different environments.

It is also important to remember when you start negotiations with your local partner that he is sending you out signals which could help you greatly in your future business dealings with him. But if you don't understand the specific context, your interpretation of these signals will probably be wrong. So high quality information is an important ingredient of success. You should always avoid thinking that your local partner is less efficient, less educated or less developed than you are. This is usually not true and even if it were, people are not stupid and they feel your attitude towards them, and this will put a strain on the business relationship.

It is essential to be flexible, open-minded and to listen. Avoid thinking that your product's presentation always fits their market. In my experience, this has rarely been the case. You have to adapt your arguments for each market.

3: Take for example selling a car in France and in Holland. In France you would be advised to emphasise the performance in terms of power and technology. In Holland, you should emphasise economy and internal space and comfort. This example, I think, illustrates perfectly the different scale of values in two countries geographically so close to each other.

4: I would now like to talk about one of our more recent activities, working in Czechoslovakia. But first of all I want to say that there is no Eastern Europe and Western Europe, because for example if Prague is in eastern Europe, then Paris is probably in southern Europe and the whole thing doesn't make much sense. However, there was a difference in orientation, experience and philosophy during the last 50 years, if we include the second World War. So on one hand, we have the so-called Western world playing the traditional role of being helpful, and on the other hand, the so-called Eastern world, complexed about their heritage of more than 40 years of communism, which means not having a good system of management, no money for investment.

Even if both sides are willing to co-operate, it is difficult to make something work. For example, we carried out some market research on the potential of the construction sector of Eastern Europe. Even though we had some very good contacts, it still took us a couple of months to establish roles – who does what – and to understand the distribution system which seemed absurd compared to our recent standards. So it is not easy, even when you speak the language perfectly or are of Czech origin as I am. There is always the barrier of no common professional reference. The main thing is don't think of the East as a bloc. The so-called Eastern bloc countries have economic, industrial, social and cultural differences. For example, people often forget that Czechoslovakia was one of the first economic world powers between the two world wars.

I would like to conclude emphasising that in general terms, you will have a better chance to succeed in business if you have a certain respect and understanding in your approach to international negotiations. You must convince your partner of your professionalism and know-how. To achieve this, you must be well-informed.

SPEAKING

1 Divide the class into small groups and ask them to read the four case studies providing help when necessary and checking that all the groups are not working on the same case. The students should then discuss what they think caused the problem or misunderstanding and prepare notes for the presentation stage. After a minimum of 15 minutes, each group should present its interpretation to the rest of the class. The other students may not agree and should be encouraged to say what they understand the problem to be. This activity should lead to a more general discussion of cross-cultural problems and their relative importance.

Students may have different interpretations for each of the cases. The following are suggested answers.

1 The American did not realise the importance of the family in this part of the world. It would have been inconceivable for the Saudi to have placed his father in the care of strangers. He therefore felt that he could not trust Mr Byrd as a business partner.

2 In this case, the American CEO had no understanding of the way the French approach business negotiations. In France, it is important to spend time on preliminary discussions before mentioning financial details. The executive did not build a proper relationship with his counterpart through an exchange of views and therefore was perceived as being overbearing.

3 The French take great pride in their food and wine and foreigners should be very wary about passing judgement on the quality of food. In this case, the Frenchmen obviously thought that the food at the restaurant did not warrant such praise, and in their view, the American revealed his lack of 'savoir faire'/'savoir vivre'.

4 There are perhaps two problems involved in this case. The first may concern the nature of the food the businesswomen served. The second involves the rituals of politeness and the relationship between men and women. In many cultures, it is considered normal to serve oneself. In the male-dominated Japanese business culture however, the guest would expect to be served, particularly in this case, where the person organising the breakfast is a woman.

ROLE PLAY

This activity will provide the students with an opportunity to practise giving and asking for advice based on the themes studied throughout the unit. The activity involves both Student A and B in detailed preparation and sufficient time should be allowed for this. The A Students should use this time to prepare all the information that they know about the country chosen (their own country or one they know well). They should go through the instructions provided, point by point, writing down the advice that they will give to the B Students. They may wish to refer back to the lead-in section for some information and you should provide help concerning vocabulary when needed or, if available, encourage them to use an English dictionary. The B Students should use this time to prepare a list of questions to ask The A Students. Check that the students are preparing properly formulated questions about specific situations, like those provided for them in the examples and not questions like: *What about the use of language?* or *Tell me about non-verbal communication* etc.

During the actual role play, go around the classroom checking that the students are using the language structures provided in the examples correctly. For example:

Student B – *How important is it to be on time for business meetings in your country?*

Student A – *I would advise you to always be on time for meetings as it is considered very unprofessional to arrive late.*

WRITING

This exercise can be given as a homework assignment, but it can also be done in class. As a class activity it can be expanded by getting the students to read out their answers and to compare them with what the other students have written. This could lead to a general class discussion on the different subjects.

Advertising and Marketing

KEY VOCABULARY

It may be useful to illustrate this vocabulary by bringing in a magazine or newspaper. Show students examples of advertisements and elicit the word *advertisement* from them. Stress that although you can have 'an advertisement', *publicity* is not countable. In addition students can identify the names of well-known advertisers and famous brands. Particular attention should be given to the difference between the countable and non-countable noun forms *advertisement* and *advertising* which are often confused. Ensure that students understand the difference in meaning and pronunciation of the words ådvertise/ådvertiser/ådvertising and advêrtisement.

LEAD-IN

1 The purpose of this section is to get students to think about the different advertising media. These include print and broadcast media, outdoor advertising (posters, hoardings, skywriting), transportation advertising (signs on public transport vehicles and in stations), point of sale advertising (window displays, stands, etc.), and other media (calendars, matchbooks, pens, etc.).

2 The aim of this informal activity is not for students to find the correct answers but to use their imagination in associating products with these slogans.

Key:

1 Amtrak trains (USA)
2 Kodacolor Film
3 Grand Gourmet Beef Dinner for dogs
4 Black and Decker automatic shut-off iron
5 EverReady personal flashlight
6 Miss Clairol haircolor
7 Panasonic portable cassette system
8 Fleischmann's light margarine
9 LaChoy sauces
10 Drum hand-rolling tobacco
11 Lipton tea bags

3 As endorsement is the theme of the reading passage, this section will help students to focus on the famous personalities who are used to advertise products in their countries. In the discussion question which follows students should say whether the celebrity and the product make a good match.

READING

1 Encourage the students to read the text quickly for specific information.

Key:

1 (Woody Allen) – g (department store)
2 (John McEnroe) – d (toothpaste)
3 (Roger Moore) – b (cigarettes)
4 (Paul Newman) – c (credit card)
5 (Arnold Schwarzenegger) – a (instant noodles)
6 (Sylvester Stallone) – f (ham)
7 (Sting) – e (beer)

2 Before the second reading you could explain that because the text is from the International Herald Tribute, it includes American expressions such as *to be leery* (paragraph 11) and to *pay top dollar* (paragraph 4).

Although it is important that the meaning of an individual word is given less attention than the global meaning of a sentence, you may wish to bear in mind that the following expressions may be problematic: *(to be) caught dead doing something (paragraph 4)/heftiest pay (paragraph 12)/lest it tarnish their image (paragraph 8).*

Key:

1	c	4	b
2	a	5	b
3	a		

VOCABULARY

1 Key:

1	to run	8	a client
2	a commercial	9	a clause
3	viewers	10	a penalty
4	a slogan	11	a spokesman
5	to promote	12	a fee
6	image	13	a status symbol
7	an attorney *	14	to plummet

* Note: The word 'attorney' is used in American English; it is perhaps best explained as being a lawyer who represents a client in legal proceedings. There is no distinction between the jobs of barrister and solicitor in US law and an attorney can both have direct relations with clients and represent them in a court of law.

2 Key:

1	client's	5	promote
2	commercials	6	clauses
3	run	7	fee(s)
4	slogan(s)		

DISCUSSION

Suggestions:

1 Advantages: immediate impact, association made between the product and the star's perceived qualities.

Disadvantages: danger that personality will be remembered instead of the product, the effectiveness of an ad may suffer if the celebrity appears in ads for different advertisers.

2/3 Free discussion questions.

LANGUAGE FOCUS

GERUND AND INFINITIVE

Focus the students' attention on the sentence from the text and use the questions to form the basis of a class discussion on the differences in usage between the gerund and infinitive.

Practice

1 Key:

1 (paragraph 5) 'Paul Newman, for instance, hums in an elevator *before letting* viewers know that Fuji Bank's credit card is his "main card".'

2 (paragraph 6) 'John McEnroe, the tennis player, and his actress wife, Tatum O'Neal, joke together in matching shirts *while holding up* a box of Assess toothpaste.'

3 (paragraph 10) 'Mr Axelrad and others protect their clients' American reputations *by demanding* that "Japan-only" clauses be written into advertising contracts.'

4 (paragraph 11) 'One company spokesman, *after* first *demanding* anonymity for himself and his firm, would only say, "Our star hates to be mentioned".'

2 Before doing this exercise, find out what the students know about Coca Cola. Where did it start? What is its product range? What image do the Coca Cola commercials give of the product and the consumers who buy it?

Key:

1	running	9	deciding
2	to make	10	to appear
3	to build/building	11	launching
4	transforming	12	changing
5	setting up	13	returning
6	to bring	14	drinking
7	to reflect	15	to expand/expanding
8	creating		

SKILLS FOCUS

SPEAKING: 1 Describing target markets.

1 This exercise encourages students to work autonomously, sharing ideas and comparing points of view.

The purpose of the activity is to generate discussion and therefore the explanations of the advertisements should not be given until after the students have given their presentations in part 2.

Advertisement 1: A more difficult advertisement to analyse as the target is not featured. The ad appeared in 'Country Living' magazine which is devoted to interior decorating and fine foods. The ad therefore appeals to a mainstream target which appreciates traditional values and good quality products. The target market is most likely made up of professional people over the age of 30 and who make a comfortable living.

Advertisement 2: This ad appeared in the American student magazine 'Spin' and is designed to attract young people who are entering university as resident students. The 'before and after' technique used in the ad shows the transformation of a cautious, conservative student whose parents probably bought the backpack for its strength and reliability. After four years of university, the student has become more fulfilled and confident, and the product has found its place as a fashionable element of his new lifestyle.

2 You may find that a discussion will develop as to why people had different ideas about the advertisements. Make sure that in each case the students explain why they made certain decisions.

SPEAKING: 2

Analysing advertisements

This exercise will give students the opportunity to make a detailed comparison of different advertisements which promote the same type of product. Although students are asked to supply their own ads, you should also have some at hand. Note that some of the most common advertising techniques used are: factual statements, product comparison, demonstration, dramatisation, endorsement and humour.

This activity could be used as a writing assignment.

LISTENING

It may be useful to pre-teach the abbreviation *cc* (as in cubic centimetres) and mention that the speaker has an American accent.

1 Key: b

Tapescript:

EXTRACT 1: Well, who buys Harley-Davidson? There's no actual Harley-Davidson customer. It is almost everybody because the motorcycle Harley-Davidson is more than ever used as a means of transportation, and it is no longer just seen as a piece of fashion. We have customers that buy a Sportster with 19 and start to go up to a 30 and 40 cc (cubic centimetres) after two or three years. But we also have the customer that at 45 years does his driving licence, and his riding licence, and buys a Harley. So there is actually no special Harley customer. The average age of the Harley-Davidson company, the buyer of the motorcycle, is I'd say about 35 years, which is higher than all the other companies, that is for sure.

2 Key:

a tradition (or history), individualism

b The marketing strategy is basically the same for all countries. Harley-Davidson managers pay close attention to what their customers have to say

Tapescript:

EXTRACT 2: Everybody knows that the mentality of the people in France is different from the mentality in Germany, but the funny thing is that the image of Harley-Davidson is the same in every country. It is the tradition, it's the individualism of the bike, it is also the history (tradition, that's what I said), it's 90 years' history.

So the general image of Harley-Davidson in all the countries is the same. But there are slight differences how the name or the philosophy is seen by people in different countries. And you cannot say I have a different marketing strategy for every country. You try to adapt slightly.

It is the only company in the world where you will find all the presidents, if there's a rally, a big HOG rally for example, our Harley Owner's Group, they are all there and they talk to the customers, they have their beer with them. Alright, the decisions are made with the customer, not upstairs in an office. Alright if you don't move from the office, you don't have any information, what the customer wants, and we produce for the customer, not for us. So this is the marketing strategy.

3 Key:

Japan, France, Germany, United Kingdom, Spain, Italy, Holland, Belgium and Austria

Tapescript:

EXTRACT 3: Japan, yeah, Japan is a little bit bigger than France, and then we have Germany, and then I think England (UK, the British market). French, German, British market, Spanish or Italian, Dutch market, Belgian market, and the smallest, right now, of the bigger markets is Austria, with I think 160 bikes.

4

Before listening to the extract students should have understood from the chart that Harley-Davidson does not export a large number of motorcycles. The mistake that Harley-Davidson made before 1981 was that they concentrated more on quantity than on quality which resulted in a loss of market share.

EXTRACT 4: When I said I like the situation we're in, that means, sure enough, on a sales point of view, that means for us, we're sold out, which is very good. But on the other hand, we have a problem with the customers because we cannot meet the demand of the motorcycles, we cannot meet the demand, the increased demand, of the accessories. We're struggling to give 'em the maximum that's possible and we are right now at 100% of production. We cannot do more. Not one bike more, without losing quality. Alright, and we don't want to lose quality. This is what happened before '81: quantity but not quality. This is why we lost the market. And this will never happen again.

U N I T   5

Franchising

KEY VOCABULARY

It is important that the students fully understand the basic terminology of franchising which contains some quite difficult terms concerning the contractual nature of the relationship between the franchisee and the franchisor. In this unit we are dealing mainly with what is known as 'Business format franchising', where the owner of a business is selling a complete package to the franchisee, enabling him or her to set up an individual operation.

LEAD-IN

1 Students should have no difficulty in finding one example for each category given the international growth of franchising over the last few years. Some additional examples have, however, been provided below:

Fast food	Clothing	Car maintenance
MacDonald's Baskin Robbins	Benetton Jacadi	Ziebart Tidy Car Midas

2 This short activity enables students to concentrate on the implications and constraints of the relationship between the franchisee and the franchisor. Allow students sufficient time to come to a decision on all nine statements and then go through them with the class as a whole:

Key:

	F'R	F'E
1		✓
2	✓	
3		✓
4		✓
5	✓	
6		✓
7		✓
8		✓
9	✓	

3 Key:

Percentage success rate:	90%
Number of people employed USA: UK:	500,000 185,000
Annual turnover USA: UK:	$400 bn £4.7 bn

Tapescript:

Franchising is not only growing, but is expanding, and certainly over the past fifteen years. What we do know is that franchising has had a much higher success rate than that of the ordinary small business sector. We do know from our surveys that nine out of ten franchises succeed.

Franchising definitely is big business, I would agree with that. In the USA half a million people are employed in it. It accounts currently for 30% of all retail sales and it is projected to reach 50% by the turn of the century. At the moment, 400 billion dollars worth of business is achieved annually. In the UK our current sales are approximately 4.7 billion per annum, and this figure is projected to grow to 11 billion by 1994. And at the moment, 185,000 people are employed in the franchising industry.

READING

1 Encourage students to read through the article, focusing on the eight statements to decide whether they are true or false.

Key:

1 False
2 True
3 True
4 False (it may be the safest way but it will also mean lower returns)
5 False (US franchisors are investing in the UK in order to prepare for European expansion)
6 False
7 False
8 False

2 The students should read the article again in order to find the information necessary to complete the table.

Key:

Company	Country of origin	Sector	Markets	
			Present	Future
Burger King	USA	Fast food	Europe	—
Jacadi	France	Clothing	France	UK
Stefanel	Italy	Clothing	Italy	Eastern Europe
Servicemaster	USA	Cleaning	UK/Germany	Other Countries
Nevada Bobs	USA	Golf	UK	Germany/France
The Body Shop	UK	Body care	Europe	—

3 Key:

Spain has the highest number with 123 outlets per franchisor. France and Italy are in joint second position with 48 outlets per franchisor and Sweden has the lowest number with only 16 outlets.

VOCABULARY

1 Encourage students to look at the words in context in order to deduce their meanings.

Key:

1	d	5	h	8	b
2	e	6	j	9	g
3	i	7	a	10	f
4	c				

2 Exercises 2 and 3 activate some of the vocabulary that students have come across in the article, encouraging them to identify and use it in both noun and verb forms.

Key:

Verb	Noun
expand	expansion
grow	growth
succeed	success
predict	prediction
forecast	forecast
exhibit	exhibition
consult	consultant
establish	establishment
operate	operator

3 Key:

1	outlet	6	exhibitions
2	operate (run)	7	operators
3	consultant	8	licence
4	expand (grow)	9	predicted (forecast)
5	established		

DISCUSSION

1 The purpose of this section is to illustrate the difference between an ordinary franchise and a master franchise where one person or company buys the rights to develop a specific business franchise within one particular country. A master franchisor acts as the intermediary between the franchisor and future franchisees and oversees the development of the business in a particular country. In the first advert, which was published in *The International Herald Tribune*, Uniglobe are offering master franchises for different countries in Europe. This type of opportunity would only be suitable for a businessperson who had the necessary capital and experience. In the second advert, which appeared in the British daily newspaper *The Daily Mail*, Uniglobe are inviting applications only for individual franchises within the United Kingdom. These franchises involve much lower capital investment and do not require the same level of business expertise.

2 This advertisement is one of a series that appeared in a highly successful international campaign that Benetton organised on behalf of all of its franchisees. It provides a good illustration of the role that the franchisor can play in promoting a company and its products. This material can also be exploited as an exercise in which students are asked to reflect about some of the ethical implications of this type of advertising. This will stimulate a lively debate and could be enlarged upon by asking if students feel this type of advertising is effective and if so, why.

LANGUAGE FOCUS

RELATIVE CLAUSES

Practice

1 Key:

	D	N
1	✓	
2		✓
3		✓
4	✓	
5		✓
6	✓	

2 Key:

1 The woman *who* introduced me to Mr Ross was Australian.

2 Have you read the report (*which/that*) I left on your desk last night?

3 The people (*who[m]*) we interviewed were very highly qualified.

4 What's the name of the man *whose* car you borrowed?

5 This is one of the videos (*which/that*) we use for training purposes.

3 Key:

1	c	4	b	7	d
2	e	5	g		
3	f	6	a		

SKILLS FOCUS

LISTENING

You may find it useful to point out that the first two speakers have American accents and speak quite quickly. The third, Klaus Ueber, speaks more slowly and with a slight northern European accent.

Name	Position	Company Name	Sector of activity	Number of outlets
John Hayes	–	Hayes Group	Promotion of franchise businesses	–
Kay Ainsley	Development Director	Domino's Pizza	Fast food	US: 5000 Non-US: 387
Klaus Ueber	Managing Director	Natural Beauty Products Ltd.	Cosmetics Toiletries	12

1 Key:

Tapescript:

SPEAKER 1: I'm John Hayes, H–A–Y–E–S. My company is the Hayes Group and we are involved in the promotion of franchise businesses internationally. Our client list includes the International Franchise Association which represents franchisors throughout the world.

SPEAKER 2: My name is Kay Ainsley and I am the Development Director International for Domino's Pizza. We're headquartered in Ann Arbor, Michigan. We have over 5,000 outlets in the US and overseas we have 387. We operate in 23 different countries around the world.

SPEAKER 3: My name is Klaus Ueber. I'm Managing Director of Natural Beauty Products Ltd. The company's based in Bridgend in Wales. And we manufacture a range of natural herbal cosmetics and toiletries which now has 500 products in its range. They're mid to lower-price points. And we've come to the Paris exhibition to launch in Europe our Body Reform specialist beauty shop franchise. At this point in time, we only have 12 totally dedicated outlets, although our products are being marketed in a number of countries, including some French territories, by independent retailers.

2 Key:

John Hayes makes no mention of the following:

what bank to deal with

what experience employees should have

which computers to use

when to close the business for a holiday

Tapescript:

For example, if you're the franchisor and I'm the franchisee, you are going to have a certain way that you want me to operate the business from A through Z, and in your operations manual you'll tell me what to wear. You'll tell me what my employees have to wear, what time I should open my business and close my business, what I, not necessarily, what I should charge, but guidelines on what I should be charging. You would tell me what to say to people and what not to say to people, what to order what not to order, who to order it from, what to sell and what not to sell. All of this is defined by you the franchisor.

3 Lead into this activity by asking the students, in pairs, to select three adjectives which they feel describe the qualities which are desirable for a franchisee. The students should then present the adjectives to the class.

Key:

1 a Because he or she will be dealing with people.
  b Are you goal-orientated?
     Does meeting targets and setting objectives appeal to you?
  c He expects the franchisee to get on with his/her part of the deal and develop the business without constant supervision.
  d He expects the franchisor to support him.

2 a dealing . . . customers
  b tend to be . . . self-starters
  c basis . . . sides . . . obligations

Tapescript:

I don't think it's anything mysterious as such. A franchisee will be dealing with customers, so therefore it's not easy for a shy and retiring person to operate in that sort of environment. Successful franchisees tend to be positive, outgoing, self-starters, able to stick to a job and see it through. We always ask potential franchisees, 'Are you goal orientated?', 'Does meeting targets and setting objectives appeal to you?'. You'll expect the franchisor team to support you; in return, the franchisor expects you to get on with your part of the deal and develop the business without constant supervision. It's the basis for a successful relationship, that mutual relationship, and the fulfilment of both sides carrying out their obligations.

SPEAKING:

In this activity students practise alternately the skills of asking for and providing specific information about a UK franchise operation. The initial role play is preceded by a short vocabulary section where potential problem words are explained and is followed by a discussion phase during which students can compare the two franchises. The main differences between the two operations lie in the levels of the franchise fees, the capital requirements and the projected profit and loss figures.

Monitor the students as they read through the information about the two franchise operations, ensuring that they understand the vocabulary and abbreviations such as *BFA* (British Franchise Association).

WRITING

Students should prepare a short and concise report highlighting only the most significant information in each chart.

U N I T   6

Japan and the Business World

LEAD-IN

1 Much emphasis is placed by the mass media on Japan's economic success and on the growing Japanese presence in the world economy. The students may therefore be familiar with some of the spectacular acquisitions made by major Japanese companies, such as Sony Corporation's acquisition of Columbia Pictures, and will undoubtedly be aware of the emotional reactions that such deals can provoke. The statements provided in this section deal with either some of the lesser known or controversial aspects of the Japanese business scene.

In groups, the students should first read and then discuss the various statements for about fifteen minutes. A spokesperson should then be selected from each group and asked to share their group's views on one or two particular statements with the rest of the class. To stimulate the debate, present conflicting points of view by asking which students see Japanese investment and acquisitions as beneficial and which students consider them a threat to the world economy. The students may also wish to make an assessment of the Japanese presence in their own countries.

2 This short task is designed to compare the hours worked in Japan with those worked in other countries. Students should be encouraged to draw upon their own knowledge of the working practices of these places to identify the numbers of hours worked. Those students whose countries are not listed may wish to tell the class how many hours are worked on average there.

Key:

1	f	**4**	a
2	c	**5**	d
3	e	**6**	b

In the class discussion that follows, some students may say that they find it unattractive to work 46.8 hours per week, but others may point out that such long working hours have made Japan a major economic power. The students will probably mention that long working hours can lead to fatigue and stress. This will help lead into the topic of the reading passage.

READING

1 Before reading the article, students should first skim through it to find the definition of *karoshi* (paragraph 1): death from overwork.

2 Key:

1	T	**4**	T
2	F	**5**	F
3	T	**6**	F

VOCABULARY

Key:

1	compensation	**5**	figures
2	shifts	**6**	overtime
3	authority	**7**	production
4	headline	**8**	poll

Note: You may wish to point out that Tom Peters is an internationally-known American business consultant.

DISCUSSION

Suggestions:

1 This discussion topic is designed to have students react to the notion of loyalty which is very strong in Japan, in so far as workers very often assimilate their employers' goals. In order to stimulate the debate, insist on some of the differences between the Japanese and the Western notions of work. Japanese firms are very group oriented and play an important economic as well as social role. The Japanese worker generally has a strong sense of mission and people readily work long hours and reduce their holiday time to ensure the success of their firm. This point will be dealt with in greater detail in the listening passages.

2 In Japan, monetary reward and holidays do not appear to be crucial aspects of one's working life when compared to the situation in Western countries. The students should discuss why they believe holidays and leisure time are important, and can compare the average time spent on holidays in their countries (for instance, it is interesting to note that 65% of the Dutch go on holiday, compared to 31% of the Portuguese).

As a further discussion point, you may wish to ask the students if there are any other countries whose work culture resembles that of Japan.

LANGUAGE FOCUS

EXPRESSING CONTRAST

Practice

Suggested answers:

1 In spite of the success of some Japanese women in business, the majority of Japanese companies are run by men.

2 Although they are dedicated to their companies, many young Japanese employees want more leisure time.

3 Despite their intense work habits, many Japanese socialise quite easily after work.

4 Even though their salaries have increased, 60% of Japanese workers still spend Saturday at work.

5 Despite some similarities in Japanese and American management practices, there are many striking differences between them.

6 The headquarters of most Japanese companies are located in Tokyo even though the rents are very expensive.

SKILLS FOCUS

MEMO WRITING

Key:

1 Date on which the memo is sent.

2 Name of the person to whom the memo is sent.

3 Name of the person sending the memo.

4 A short heading, which tells you what the memo is about.

5 A brief introduction to the memo giving the most important information.

6 The 'body' of the memo, usually divided into numbered paragraphs which develop the information.

7 The conclusion of the memo, which often recommends a course of action.

8 Unlike letters, the memo does not contain forms of address (such as Dear Ms X) or the sender's signature. The sender usually types his or her name or initials at the end of the memo.

LISTENING 1

1 Divide the class into pairs before you play the recording. Although the speaker has a distinct Japanese accent, she does speak slowly and clearly. Stop the cassette briefly at the points given in the tapescript so that the students can organise their notes.

Tapescript:

I'm very glad to see you are interested in learning more about Japan, because you will never be able to do business with the Japanese unless you understand some basic aspects of Japanese management and Japanese corporate culture in general.

In my seminars, I usually talk about three fundamental principles of Japanese management. The first is the emphasis on the group in Japanese corporations. The second is the importance of human or interpersonal relationships. And the last point I discuss is the role of Japanese managers as generalists and facilitators.

All right then, we'll talk about, briefly, these three principles. The first point then, the emphasis on the group. This group orientation manifests itself in a following example (you can yourself conduct this experiment). If you ask any Japanese businessman what he does, he will almost invariably answer by saying, 'I am a Sony man', or 'I work for Mitsubishi', or 'I'm with such and such company', instead of telling you, if he's a whether he's an engineer or an accountant, for instance, you see.

This point, the emphasis on the group, the group orientation explains the other two principles as well. For instance, Japan is geographically an island. It's an island nation, it's like a boat with an overcrowded and homogeneous population. This explains partially already why this group orientation is so important and also necessary for the very survival of Japan and Japanese corporations as well. You see, by the way, the people are the only resource Japan possesses. It is an island nation without other natural resources. So it's the question of survival also.

Teacher: short pause here

That leads us to the second question, the second emphasis rather, namely the emphasis on human or interpersonal factors or relationships. In this overcrowded island nation, in order to achieve or survive together, they have to learn, like I said, to get along, and in order to achieve this, there are certain things they have to learn, like harmony. How do you achieve harmony? By sacrificing a little bit of self-interest for the sake of the group. And also by compromising, by trying to have everybody agree, namely, to achieve or to arrive at the consensus of the group, you see.

Once you are employed, or hired by the company, you remain with this company until your retirement, the so-called 'lifetime employment'. That explains a lot of things already, like seniority order, because you enter the company along with your peers, the same age group. You graduated from the university together, so you get promoted together, and so you climb this company, organizational ladder, little by little together, slowly but steadily.

Teacher: short pause here

The last and the third point or principle is a view of managers or executives as generalists and facilitators, rather than decision-makers.

In general, in a Japanese corporation, everybody is more or less trained to be a generalist rather than a specialist. Even if you are an engineer, when you have just joined the company, you will have this orientation and you will be transferred from one department to the other and you'll be rotated in every department of the company to familiarise yourself with the entire company and for instance, since you are not narrowly specialising in one field, you can take over somebody else's role.

I also talk about 'ringisho', the so-called 'ringisho', usually translated as 'the management by consensus'. That means that all the employees participate in the process of decision making. They form small groups in each department and they discuss the matter with each other. They arrive at an agreement, the consensus, and then the departmental chief or the executive will have to agree himself or herself. And this way, the consensus is achieved. Everybody is involved in the process. It's not like, say, an American way of decision making by one big executive or the president.

This is just a brief description of my seminars, but I think if you attend them, I can give you even more insight into Japanese corporate culture, which I think will help you greatly in your coming business trip to Japan.

2 After the students have compared information, go around to each group and check the students' notes to see which passages they found the most difficult and to draw their attention to specific details that they may have overlooked.

WRITING

This writing activity should take approximately twenty minutes. As the students work, go around to each group to make sure the instructions for memo writing are being followed. Collect the memos at the end of the session in order to correct possible mistakes in style, grammar and spelling.

Suggested answer:

MEMO

To: Philip Groves, Managing Director

From: Vincent Mills, Human Resources Manager

Date: March 29, 1994

Subject: Japanese culture and management seminars

I met Ms Moriwake, the Japanese consultant, who summarised the three main themes of her seminars.

1 The emphasis on the group is very important in Japanese corporations (i.e. a person will tell you the company he works for instead of the job he does). Also, as an island nation without natural resources, people must learn to get along with each other. This is necessary for the survival of Japanese corporations.

2 Human relationships are also discussed in the seminars. To achieve harmony, people make sacrifices for the sake of the group and try to agree with each other. Lifetime employment is also common. Employees of the same age who are hired together also get promoted together until retirement.

3 Finally, in Japanese corporations everyone is trained to be a generalist and can therefore take over several different duties. Management by consensus is also common. Decisions are made by all employees and not just by one top executive.

I believe our executives should attend these seminars. A better understanding of Japanese culture and management will certainly help them in the negotiations in Japan.

VM

LISTENING 2

1 Key:

Tips for doing business with the Japanese

Topic	Recommendation	Reason(s)
Age of executives	Young men should not be sent to conduct business negotiations.	• Seniority is important in lifetime employment system. • Japanese top executives are much older than American ones. • It is an insult to the Japanese to do business with young people.
The business card	Have about 200 bilingual cards printed.	• Every business encounter starts with the exchange of a business card.
Socialising	Make sure it is all right to bring your wife when socialising	• The Japanese business world is almost exclusively masculine. • Men don't bring their wives when socialising.
Business meetings and negotiations	Don't talk too much and don't expect 'yes' or 'no' answers.	• Japanese culture is essentially non-verbal. • It takes time to make a decision.

Tapescript:

Let me give you a few practical tips on doing business with the Japanese. First of all for instance, age is a very important factor. In this type of system where lifetime employment is practised, seniority becomes very important as you can see. Japanese top executives, for instance, are much older than their American counterparts. So, many American companies fail in doing business with Japan or with the Japanese by sending far too young men to conduct business negotiations in Japan with their Japanese counterparts, who could be their fathers! It is already quite an insult to the Japanese.

The next tip might be the business card. The business card is not a simple piece of paper in Japan. Every business encounter starts with the exchange of business cards. The business card is the person himself. So, you offer one and he will offer you one. You receive it with reverence, you study it carefully and put it away in your wallet with utmost care. So, the first thing you should do as soon as you've arrived in Japan is to have about 200 bilingual business cards printed for yourself.

Another tip is on socializing. You see, the Japanese business world is almost exclusively masculine. Men don't bring their wives when they're socializing. So, make absolutely sure beforehand if it's all right to bring your wife. Otherwise, it could be a very embarrassing situation.

The last tip I can give you is about a business meeting or a negotiation. First of all, don't talk too much. It's essentially a non-verbal culture. And don't expect the Japanese businessman to answer you in clear 'yes' or 'no', because it sounds too confrontational, and it takes time in this consensus-oriented system to make a decision, to arrive at the decision.

So, always keep in mind that the Japanese culture is radically different from yours.

2 Free discussion questions.

Business and the Environment

LEAD-IN

1 The lead-in section presents the students with a selection of cartoons which depict some of the environmental problems we are facing in the world today. They were published in World Press Review and were part of an exhibition entitled 'Our Endangered Planet' held in Moscow in 1990. Before discussing the cartoons, the students will need to be introduced to the basic vocabulary of the environment. This can be done by asking the students to talk about the various environmental problems which they consider to be important. Write any difficult or technical words on the blackboard as they come up. For example, the students will need to be familiar with such terms as *ozone layer*, *global warming*, *oil spills*, *chemical waste*, *nuclear waste* and *pollution*. Group the various environmental threats under headings such as *air pollution* and *water pollution*.

Once this has been done the students can then start discussing the cartoons in small groups. They are asked to identify which environmental threats the cartoons refer to, as well as to select the one which they find to be the most effective. Each group is also asked to discuss what they consider to be the most important environmental causes today. Go around the classroom checking that the students are actually discussing the cartoons and describing how they present the problem visually and not simply labelling each one, for example, *This one deals with air pollution and this one with water pollution*.

They should be encouraged to describe each one in detail. In the case of the first cartoon, the students could discuss how our perception of the world has changed through the ages, for example *We used to think the world was flat, then it was thought to be square. It was finally discovered to be round and nowadays we could see it as being a rubbish bin*.

They should also say why they think certain cartoons are more effective than others, for example, is it better to use humorous or shocking images to communicate an environmental message? When each group has correctly completed the activity, invite individual groups to present their interpretations and opinions to the rest of the class. This should lead to a more general discussion about the importance of the environmental threats depicted in the cartoons. Encourage students to discuss the environmental awareness campaigns in their own countries.

2 As the students have been introduced to the general vocabulary relating to the environment in Lead-in 1, they are now asked to discuss the role that business can play in environmental concerns. Three statements are provided as a basis for the discussion. Before reading these statements, ask the students if they have ever read or heard about companies being sued or rewarded for their policies concerning the environment. They may have heard about the Exxon Valdez tanker which caused a major oil slick in Alaska, or they may have seen advertisement campaigns based on a company's contribution to the environment, for example, washing powder 'without phosphates' or catalytic converters for cars.

READING

Before students read the text, write *The Body Shop* on the board and ask them if they have heard of it. If so, what does this name mean to them?

Key:

1   The first demonstration mentioned in the text refers to the one organized by environmental activist groups. There were twenty people present and they attracted little or no publicity. The second one mentioned, refers to the Body Shop demonstration where two hundred and fifty people gathered outside the Brazilian embassy in London to protest about the same cause. This demonstration attracted worldwide media interest, and The Body Shop and its franchisees contributed hundreds of thousands of dollars to the cause. The event organised by The Body Shop attracted more attention because it had the financial backing of a big business.

2   People in the UK are not surprised by this activism because The Body Shop has been campaigning for various community and environmental projects for many years now.

3   The Trade Not Aid programme is designed to create employment, by exploiting local resources and skills in developing countries, rather than simply giving money through charities.

4   According to Anita Roddick, magazine articles saying Princess Diana uses Body Shop products provide the best type of publicity to increase sales.

5   The fact that Anita Roddick involves her employees in her environmental policies gives them the feeling of belonging to a socially responsible organisation which can change things. This means that she has enthusiastic and motivated sales teams which in the long run helps to increase sales and profits.

VOCABULARY

1 Key:

1	issues	5	fund-raising
2	campaigns	6	displays
3	mobilising	7	audience
4	petition	8	publicity

2 Key:

1	d	3	a	5	b
2	c	4	e		

3 The objective of this exercise is to test students' comprehension of phrases which they may be unfamiliar with by asking students to use them in sentences.

Key:

1   The government is waging a campaign against all forms of discrimination.
2   Her plans grabbed the imagination of the entire company.
3   I would like to draw the following facts to your attention.
4   Money played a major role in my decision to accept the job.
5   The report raised a question about his ability to do the job.

4 Key:

1	remote	6	links
2	worldwide	7	profits
3	defense	8	admit
4	no longer	9	random
5	set up	10	excitement

Note: The British English spelling of defense (paragraph 2) is defence.

DISCUSSION

Through these three discussion questions the students are asked to give their opinion of The Body Shop's policy and to talk about companies involved in similar projects in their own country. Questions about the motivation behind the socially aware policies of companies such as The Body Shop are often asked in relation to such organisations. Introduce this as a further discussion point. Is The Body Shop's 'corporate activism' merely a very clever marketing ploy?

LANGUAGE FOCUS

THE PASSIVE

Practice

1 Key:

1	is extracted, are used	5	are arranged, (are) transported
2	is heated	6	are returned, are removed
3	are filled, (are) labelled	7	are ground
4	are added	8	are produced

2 Key:

1   Peppermint foot lotion was introduced specially for the London marathon.
2   New products will be made in the Soapworks factory in future.
3   A product can be discontinued if it is not successful.
4   Information about how consumers should use the product is given on detailed labels.
5   Before entering the American market, a strong image had already been established in the UK.
6   More than 30 items have recently been added to The Body Shop product range.

7 Body Shop products are not tested on animals.
8 Plastic bottles may be returned for refilling.

DESCRIBING GROUPS AND SUBGROUPS

Practice

1 Key:

1	most	4	two
2	none	5	All
3	half	6	a few

2 During the first step of this activity, go around the classroom helping the groups to prepare their presentations and checking that they have fully understood the language of groups and subgroups. They should be making sentences like: *All of us have watched a TV documentary about the environment, two of us are members of an environmental association, none of us has ever bought a Body Shop product.* Check that students have understood the word *graduate* (a person who has studied at a higher level for three or four years, often at a university, and who has received a Bachelor's degree).

SKILLS FOCUS

SPEAKING

The purpose of this exercise is to stimulate thought and discussion, and students should be encouraged to come up with their own solutions to these problems which they can then present to the class. After the presentations have been made, it may be useful to tell students the following information about what action was actually taken by the companies involved.

1 Procter and Gamble introduced concentrated fabric softener in small refill packs to reduce packaging to a minimum.
2 General Motors have designed a nonpolluting electric car. The car produces no toxic emissions and can run for 125 miles before the battery needs to be recharged. (The students may mention catalytic converters.)
3 Goodyear promotes recycling of used tyres as an energy source.
4 Kodak offers film developers a financial incentive to return used cameras for re-use or recycling.
5 HJ Heinz insists that the fishermen cast their nets deeper into the sea where the dolphins do not swim.
6 Empire Berol USA now makes pencils from a more common wood, incense cedar, found in the USA.

LISTENING

1 During this first listening activity the students are asked to listen for quite a lot of specific information, therefore they will need to hear the extract more than once. Point out that the people they will hear are authentic speakers who were interviewed in a Body Shop in London, and therefore use a very conversational speaking style and sometimes speak quickly. The students should be encouraged to take notes while listening and to use these notes to complete the table. Once they have done this, ask the students what they think of the reasons given by the speakers and if their own buying decisions are based on the same kinds of considerations.

Key:

Customers	Reasons for buying Body Shop products
1	This customer buys Body Shop products because she is against testing on animals and also because she feels that The Body Shop is having a good effect on the environment.
2	Body Shop products suit this customer's skin.
3 & 4	These customers appreciate the lack of packaging and the fact that products are not tested on animals.
5	This customer finds the shops themselves pleasant to shop in, and also likes the way products are presented and packaged.
6	This customer likes the quality of the products and thinks they make good presents.
7	The price and the packaging correspond to this customer's demands.
8	This customer buys the products for their established brand name and good reputation.

Tapescript

CUSTOMER 1: Because I believe that nothing should be tested on animals and I believe what they do must be having some good effect on the environment, so that's why I buy them.

CUSTOMER 2: Because as I've said, I've been using it for ten years (most of their products for ten years), and they suit my skin and skin type.

CUSTOMERS 3 & 4: I think that's the major part of it, not testing, and the lack of packaging. It makes the choice easier rather than having to read gallons and gallons of packaging. You have a guarantee that it's not tested on animals as well, because other places they tell you, but you're not quite sure.

CUSTOMER 5: Well I like the shops, I think they're very nice, so it's a nice place to be. So probably that really, the presentation, the packaging, the sort of ideas behind the whole thing.

CUSTOMER 6: The stuff's good, and also the packaging's very nice for presents.

CUSTOMER 7: Economic reasons (generally they're a fairly reasonable price). Like the packaging – simple, less waste.

CUSTOMER 8: I suppose, you know, the name is quite well established and so you go for something that obviously somebody else has tried before you, you know.

2 Play each extract separately pausing between each extract in order to give the students time to organize their notes. They should then use their notes to write full answers like those provided in the key below.

Key:

Companies will have to pay closer attention to environmental matters in future if they want to recruit the best employees, continue to attract new customers and avoid problems with the regulatory bodies.

The Body Shop minimises packaging and provides a refill service which promotes recycling. They also take special care to use plastics that are readily recyclable for their packaging.

Tapescript:

EXTRACT 1: There's also a strong interest on the part of the consumers or clients, increasingly, particularly the younger generation has an attitude which is very critical of industries which do not take their environmental responsibility seriously. And so, again, if you want to attract custom, if you want to attract, indeed the best employees in the future, you're going to have to be a company which recognizes the responsibility to manage your environmental impact and to minimize your environmental impact as far as you possibly can. For regulatory reasons and for commercial reasons, there will be no option but to embrace environmentalism in a much more comprehensive way in the future.

EXTRACT 2: The Body Shop can play an important role in helping demonstrate that an industry or a business can be both financially and commercially successful and take its responsibilities for environmental management seriously as well.

A big issue for the Body Shop at the moment is packaging and we very much welcome the direction of European legislation on packaging. We feel very strongly that retailers should take absolute responsibility for its consumer waste and not just rely on local government to collect and sort packaging waste. So we are very keen to make sure that our packaging is first minimised in terms of the quantities that we use. Hence we promote refill service, we promote recycling. But we also need to make sure that our materials that we use for packaging are very readily recyclable, so we are trying to move into just a few plastics to make sure that if we receive those back to a central point in each country, they are readily recyclable. So we're particularly keen to push for better practices on recycling and packaging generally.

WRITING

This exercise is designed to be a homework assignment. The students are asked to look at labels and packaging to find the equivalent in their own language for the following kinds of words and expressions: *natural, petroleum-free, pesticide-free, plant-based, cruelty-free, energy-efficient, low-fume, non-*

toxic, non-corrosive, recyclable, reusable, compostable, biodegradable. They are then required to write a short composition about whether environmental concerns affect their purchasing decisions or not. Encourage students to think about price as well. Do they think eco-friendly products are more expensive and if so, are they as consumers willing to pay the difference? The compositions can be read out during the next class and compared with those of the other students. Collect them afterwards so that they can be corrected in more detail.

Retailing

KEY VOCABULARY

This section provides a simplified description of the retail sector in the United Kingdom and explains briefly how the industry is classified according to the different types of operations. Terms such as *wholesaling*, *co-operatives* and *cash and carry* may be introduced at this stage in order to provide students with more information about the retail trade. Encourage students to give examples of businesses from their own countries which fall into the retail categories explained in this section.

LEAD-IN

1 Here students are asked to think about how the retail trade is organised in their own countries and to consider what types of products are sold by their major retailers. In this way they will be able to focus on some of the key points that Dr Burt will be describing in the listening section that follows.

2 Key:

	UK	Continental Europe
Pricing	Non-competitive	Competitive
Margins of food retailers	High	Low
Types of stores and products sold	No hypermarkets only food super-stores	True hypermarkets selling food and non-food products
Management of retail businesses	Professional	Considerable family influence

Tapescript:

I think there's two or three clear differences. Perhaps the most obvious is the absence of price competition in most of UK retailing. Any of us who have bought food products in particular in foreign countries will notice that pricing is very different. In most countries in continental Europe, retailers compete on price, the discounts are part of the promotional policy and if we actually look at the margins that the companies make in the two countries or the two areas, in the UK food retailers have a margin of about 5 to 6%, and in France and Germany, for example, it's much closer to 1%.

Another main difference I think is that the UK does not really have hypermarkets in the continental sense. We tend to have food superstores that sell food only, yet when you get into France, Germany and Spain, there are true hypermarkets, much larger units, which not only sell food, but a whole range of non-food products, going into clothing, selling refrigerators, books and a whole range of non-food products, and this is not the case in the UK. In the UK, we have developed specialists that sell the refrigerators and that sort of non-food material separately.

I think one of the main competitive advantages of UK retailers is certainly their professional management attitudes. In the UK, most retailers, if not all retailers, are now professionally managed rather than being managed by families. In the continent, the same trend is under way, but we still have considerable family influence in businesses in most countries.

READING

Before the students read the text, encourage them to focus on the headline 'Richer pickings', and sub-headline. What do they understand by it? Encourage students to use an English dictionary if they do not understand the word *pickings*. Why do the students think that the name 'Richer Sounds' was chosen as the name of the retail chain?

Key:

1	b	**3**	b	**5**	c
2	c	**4**	a	**6**	a

VOCABULARY

1 Key:

1	noun	**4**	verb	**7**	noun
2	adjective	**5**	noun		
3	verb	**6**	noun		

2 Key:

1	compact disc	**4**	special offer
2	distribution system	**5**	leading name
3	mass market	**6**	sales pitch

3 Key:

1	h	**4**	e*	**7**	a
2	i	**5**	b	**8**	d
3	f	**6**	c	**9**	g

*Note: 'Turnover' is also used to mean the value of goods or services that a company has sold during a particular period of time.

4 Introduce this exercise by asking the students what they know about Marks and Spencer. Do they know what sort of a retailer they are, what they sell, what sort of image they have?

Key:

1 retailer
2 sales pitch
3 range
4 suppliers
5 leading name
6 profit

DISCUSSION

The excerpts from the catalogue make it clear that customer service is one of Richer Sounds' priorities. The six short texts with their simple and direct headlines tell the customer exactly what he or she can expect from Richer Sounds: personal attention, helpful sales assistants, information about the company itself and about hi-fi products and also 'extras' such as umbrellas which personalise the service that the company is offering. In addition to this, Richer Sounds runs a freepost service to encourage its customers to write in with their own suggestions and comments.

Use the example of this company to ask your students to think about the quality of customer service in their own country and to explain whether or not they consider this to be an important fact when choosing where to make a purchase. Students' attitudes to this question will vary widely according to nationality and culture.

LANGUAGE FOCUS

MAKE AND DO

Make and do create many problems for foreign speakers of English and although in a high number of cases the expressions simply have to be learned, it may be useful to refer students to the Grammar Reference section at the back of the book in order to provide them with some guidelines.

Practice

1 Key:

Make	Do
a suggestion	business
a decision	nothing
a mistake	an exam
a complaint	research
a speech	damage
a sound	the typing
a trip	a job
a loss	your best

2 Key:

1 making . . . decision
2 have done research
3 doing business
4 complaint was made
5 made . . . loss

LOCATING OBJECTS

1	at the top	8	next to
2	on the right	9	below
3	at the bottom	10	behind
4	in the middle	11	inside
5	On the left	12	above
6	at the back	13	between
7	at the front	14	in front of

SKILLS FOCUS

LISTENING

1 Key:

1 d **2** e **3** g **4** c **5** b **6** f **7** h **8** a

Tapescript:

This store, like all our other ones, follows a standard design. For example, the main entrance is always on the left because our research has shown that customers prefer to enter stores on the left and then they have a natural reflex to move to the right.

Fresh fruit and vegetables are always just inside the entrance. This is important because it gives a healthy image to the store.

The meat counter, however, is at the back of the store. There are two reasons for this, the first one being that meat requires a preparation and storage area. The other is that meat is an item that shoppers come to buy regularly and having it here means that they will see many other products on their way.

Likewise, basic products are rarely found next to each other. In this store, for instance, the coffee is in the first aisle, about half way down on the right, whereas the sugar is over in the fourth aisle at the end nearest the checkout.

Breakfast cereal is in the second aisle, and you'll notice that the shelf at the top contains the lesser-known brands of cereals. But the shelf just below it, which is at eye level and generates the highest sales, is reserved for the more famous brands of cereals.

The four television screens that you can see above the demonstration area are showing items that we are discounting at the moment. We have found that displaying products this way can increase sales of certain items by as much as 900%!

2 Key:

1 Customers prefer to enter on the left and then move naturally to the right.

2 This gives customers a healthy impression of the store as soon as they enter.

3 Since customers buy meat regularly they have to go past many items before getting to the meat counter.

4/5 In this way customers are brought into contact with many products as they shop for such basic things as coffee and sugar.

6 Products placed at eye-level sell best.

7 TV promotions of products can increase sales.

SPEAKING:

This activity is designed both to get students to think about their own consumer buying habits and also to make them aware of some of the criteria that have to be considered when locating a business. Encourage the A students to examine in detail how they reached the decision to buy their particular product. For example: were the motives for making this purchase personal or social? Is it the type of product that their peers would like to possess? Did they select the product for its brand name? Was there any bargaining involved? What was the atmosphere like in the shop? etc.

Ensure that student B's questionnaire contains a mixture of questions that will reveal both the facts concerning student A's purchase (how much did he or she pay for it? etc.) and also the underlying motives for buying this particular item (did buying this product affect Student A's status in any way?).

WRITING

Students should study these portraits carefully to see what clues they contain about these people's lifestyles. The clothing, the context and the body language will all give students some indication of their backgrounds, income levels and tastes. However, when students come to do the actual writing they should feel free to add and invent as much information as they can concerning how they think these people spend their money and time. Suggest that students avoid going into too much detail concerning their professional activities and concentrate more on their leisure pursuits and their behaviour as consumers.

Banking

KEY VOCABULARY

This section gives an overview of the banking system in the United Kingdom and explains some of the major differences between the various institutions that operate in this sector. This outline can be used as an introduction and then, if necessary, the specific roles of these institutions, can be described in greater detail. Check that students are conversant with some of the more specific vocabulary (*deposit, merger, loan acquisition* etc.) by writing it on the board and eliciting explanations from the students.

LEAD-IN

1 This short pairwork activity gives students the chance to discuss the different services that banks in their country make available and also to see which of these they actually use. While the class is working on the first part of this activity, go round the class offering assistance to those students who may have difficulty finding the correct English terms for some of the services such as *savings accounts* and *mortgages*. It might be useful to introduce some of the more common banking vocabulary at this stage, such as *overdraft, withdrawal, pay in* and *deposit* which students will encounter later in the unit.

2 Key:

Location: Belsize Park, north London

Number of customers: Approximately 2,500

Opening hours: 9.30-4.30 Monday-Friday

Services offered: Lending requirements and depositing money for gaining interest, safe custody, foreign money, insurance and investments.

Number of employees: 10

Role in the community: Meet requirements of customers and non-customers in the previously mentioned services.

The comparison between this bank and a bank in the students' countries should reveal some significant differences concerning such things as opening hours, the availability of interest bearing current accounts and the use of automated banking systems.

Tapescript:

My name's Peter Milson, I'm the manager of the Midland Bank at Belsize Park which is a north London suburb. I've been in the bank for 32 years, although I've only just joined this branch this week. At this branch we have approximately 2,500 customers and our basic opening hours are Monday to

Friday 9.30 to 4.30. Although some of the branches do open on a Saturday morning, there is no counter service offered at those. The main services that we offer are to customers for lending requirements and depositing money for gaining interest, safe custody, foreign money for holidays etc., insurance and investments. At this branch we have ten members of staff which in Midland size is a small to medium size branch, and our role in the community is to meet customers' and non-customer requirements in the previously mentioned services.

3 Key:

1 j chequebook
2 h bank statement
3 d credit card or debit card
4 e bill
5 g traveller's cheques
6 a bank notes
7 c coins
8 f keyboard
9 b screen
10 i cash machine (ATM)

4 Key:

1 a bank statement
2 traveller's cheques/bank notes
3 a bill
4 chequebook (a cheque)
5 credit card or debit card (or cash machine)

READING

This text is an extract from a Bank of Scotland brochure presenting HOBS (Home and Office Banking System). This brochure is designed to inform both business and private customers of some of the advantages of using the Bank of Scotland's new system. The text is written in a style that is both simple and direct and which can be easily understood by members of the general public. However, it may be useful to check that the students here understood some of the more difficult phrasal verbs which appear in the text such as *carry out* (line 4), *take up* (line 28) and *set off* (line 66).

In addition to this, draw attention to the following expressions: *no matter where you live* (line 31) and *so much for banking hours* (line 64).

The study of the HOBS system can also serve as an introduction to the vocabulary of computing in English for students to whom it is relevant. You may wish to explain the names for the different parts of a computer (*keyboard*, *printer*, *screen* or *visual display unit*, *central processing unit* and *disk drive*) and also some of the more common verbs and nouns associated with this technology. List A opposite gives the computer-related vocabulary that appears in the text and List B provides some other terms which could be introduced at this stage.

A to view, on-screen, to access, keyboard, screen, PC, memory, link.

B (to) input, data, word-processing, data-processing, to print, software, hardware, data base, spreadsheet.

1 Key:

1	T	5	F
2	F	6	T
3	F	7	T
4	F	8	F

2 Key:

Only sentences 2 and 6 contain information which appears in the text.

3 The HOBS system offers a lot of advantages and students should be able to identify at least five of these. A complete list is provided below:

With HOBS the customer can:

– have instant access to an account.
– view previous transactions.
– transfer between accounts.
– order statements and chequebooks.
– pay regular bills.
– benefit from flexible banking hours.
– access the system from anywhere in the UK.
– save money on bank charges.
– see what cleared balances are (only for subscribers to the cash management service).
– earn high interest (only for subscribers to the HOBS investment account).

DISCUSSION

1 **Suggested Answer:** The development of the HOBS system will help the Bank of Scotland to stay abreast of modern technological developments while at the same time increasing the efficiency of its banking services and freeing tellers of many routine tasks.

2 Such systems are becoming more widespread and most students will be aware of similar operations in their own countries.

VOCABULARY

1 Key:

1	m	6	l	11	b
2	i	7	d	12	k
3	h	8	f	13	j

4 a	**9** e	**14** c
5 g	**10** n	

2 Key:

1	account	6	payment
2	deposit	7	debit card
3	cheque	8	credit
4	debit	9	transactions
5	cash	10	balance

LANGUAGE FOCUS

ALLOW/ENABLE/LET

Practice

Suggested answers:

1 A fax machine allows you to transmit and receive copies of documents rapidly.
2 A portable computer lets you work while you are travelling.
3 A modem enables computers to exchange data.
4 A car phone lets you make and receive phone calls while you are in your car.
5 A credit card allows you to buy goods on credit.

FIRST AND SECOND CONDITIONAL

Practice

1 The aim of this exercise is to remind students of the difference in meaning between the first two conditionals and their structures.

Key:

1	I will have	4	will change
2	would inform	5	will open
3	would ask	6	will I receive

2 This activity should be conducted as a conversation where Student A starts by explaining the first problem and Student B then responds with his or her suggestions. Encourage each of these mini-conversations to develop freely. The students who are being given advice should say whether they think this advice is appropriate or not, for example, *Yes, but if I did that then I wouldn't be able to . . .* There are no suggested answers here and it is left up to the students to say how they would approach these particular problems. When the students have discussed each problem, bring the class together and review a sample of the suggestions that were made.

SKILLS FOCUS

SPEAKING

It is important that the A students should first decide what their priorities are; investing long term or short term. Once they have considered this they can then draw up a list of the questions that they will need to ask in order to obtain precise information about the different services provided by Lombard Bank. Go round the class to make sure that these questions are correctly phrased.

For the B students it is essential that they read their instructions very carefully and then study the document in detail, making sure that they have fully understood how each of the accounts differ and what conditions each can offer for a given investment. Go round the class answering any questions that the students may have concerning this document. Once this stage has been completed, encourage the B Students to anticipate the types of questions that a potential customer (Student A) might ask them.

Remind the B students that, as representatives of the bank, they are trying to make a sale and they should therefore be as persuasive and helpful as they can during the role play.

When students have completed the role play, bring the activity to a close by asking several of the A students to explain briefly to the class how they decided to invest their money.

LISTENING

The speaker has a very strong French accent which makes comprehension of this passage quite difficult. Point this out to the students and ask them to listen for specific examples of words that are pronounced in a French way.

1 Key:

1 A TV production company
2 Paris
3 He has worked in banks in France and Germany and as financial director for various companies in France.

Tapescript:

I'm Alain Depussé and I'm 49 years old. My first job was with a bank in France and then with a bank in Germany. Afterwards I worked for various companies as financial director in different sectors in France. I'm currently with a TV production company in Paris.

2 Ensure that the students have grasped the meaning of the terms *balance sheet* and *annual report* as these are featured in this extract. The exercise itself should be done in two parts: students first listen and complete part a) and then the tape is played again and they complete part b).

Key:

Services provided by bank	Information provided by company
1 cheap credit	1 balance sheets
2 lowest possible cost	2 annual reports
3 fast answers	3 minimum information
4 reliable officers	
5 reliable commitments	

The speaker states that only the minimum information, or information which shows the company in a good light, should be given. Nothing which could be crucial to the company's strategy should be revealed.

Tapescript:

Well, first I'll tell you what I think a bank, a commercial bank should provide a company. First is cheap credit, second is lowest possible cost of services . . . you also expect good services, fast answers and reliable officers for the day to day relationship with your banks and … last you want reliable commitments which means that the lines of credit which are confirmed to you have to be available and this is a very important factor.

On the other side it's fair to provide the banks with some information on the company. You have to give them balance sheets and annual reports but you provide them with, let's say, the minimum information or the information which makes the company appear in the best light to get best possible credit rating and therefore the lowest cost but you don't go further than that and you don't give details which could be important for your strategy.

3 Make sure that the students have read the instructions in their books and that they are aware that this extract deals only with the relationship between a company and a merchant bank. Since this is quite a difficult passage it should be played several times. During the first listening the students should be trying to understand the general sense of what Mr Depussé says about this relationship. Once this has been assimilated, students can then go on to do the second, more detailed listening task.

Key:

1 The main difference is that in this case the bank will be given very precise and up to date information about all aspects of the company.

2	a	Y		d	N
	b	Y		e	Y
	c	N			

Tapescript:

No, as I said, we don't deal with a merchant bank in the same way as a commercial bank, they, if you want to get a very good service from your merchant banker you have to give him real information, up to date, and even the future trends even if they are not good for your company so that he could advise you properly. He is basically someone to talk to about risk analysis, about market information because a good merchant banker is aware of your business and takes the initiative to warn you of dangers coming up or what competitors could be doing. What you expect also from your merchant bank is advice, discussion about ways of raising capital, of issuing shares, of making special financial packages, advice on foreign currency risk and also a third and important aspect of the relationship with the merchant bank is that when you are looking for a partner or for a strategic alliance you'll discuss it with the merchant banker and he will give you advice, eventually bring your partners or give you information and help you on the financial engineering of the deal . . . so it is fairly important and secret information which you have to give to your merchant banker and you expect from him a very true and important service.

WRITING

In this exercise students are asked to prepare a letter of complaint. Before assigning it, remind students of some of the conventions which apply to the letter form in English and briefly explain what a letter of complaint is, pointing out some of the difficulties that are involved in writing this type of correspondence. The students should realise that the tone of the letter is particularly important as this must be sufficiently direct but without being shocking. It is essential that the reasons for the complaint should be expressed as clearly and simply as possible and also that the course of action that the writer wishes to see taken be clearly indicated. The actual wording of the students' letters will obviously vary depending on how serious they consider the bank's mistakes to be.

Suggest to students that they organise their letters in three different parts:

1 *an introduction,* in which the writer should identify him/herself and give the reason(s) for writing.
2 *the main body of the letter,* where the writer explains the problem and gives a short history of how it arose.
3 *a concluding paragraph,* saying what action the writer is expecting as a result of his or her letter.

The sample letter below is intended to demonstrate how a complaint letter might be written. Show students this letter after they have completed their own, to prevent them from sticking too closely to its contents.

The Stock Exchange

Charles Colwell
24 Dundas Street
London SW1 9FZ
Nov. 6th

Mr Smith
Branch Manager
National Savings Bank
509 Wellington Street
London SW1V 9AW

Dear Mr Smith

Following the recent telephone conversation that I had with Ms Henry, I am confirming in writing the complaint that I made to her concerning the £30 overdraft charge that your bank has mistakenly debited from my account.

As you may remember, approximately one month ago I arranged for the transfer of £500 from my savings account to my current account. Unfortunately your bank gave exactly the opposite instructions, transferring instead £500 from my current account to my savings account, with the result that my current account became overdrawn. When I realised that mistake had been made I contacted you personally and you assured me that the situation would be rectified immediately and that no overdraft charge would be made.

On receiving my latest statement I was therefore most surprised to see that my current account had indeed been debited by £30 for overdraft charges. Although the transfer of the funds has now been credited to the correct account, I see no reason why I should pay a penalty as a result of a mistake made by your bank, especially as I had your personal guarantee that this would not be the case.

I have been a customer of your bank for several years now and have had, to date, no reason to complain about the quality of the services provided. However, I feel that in the present circumstances this situation should be clarified immediately and I expect a full explanation of these mistakes. Failing this, I will have no alternative but to consider transferring my accounts to another bank.

Yours sincerely,

C. Colwell

Charles Colwell

KEY VOCABULARY

This section provides a basic introduction to the stock exchange. As most of the key terms reappear in the reading passage, present the theme more generally, by asking students if they can explain what the Stock Exchange is or how it works. Isolated vocabulary such as *stocks*, *Wall Street* or *golden boys* should be encouraged. If there has been a particularly relevant development in one of the world's stock exchanges, use this as a departure point for discussion. Once this has been done, the class can read through the key vocabulary passage.

LEAD-IN

The purpose of this section is to introduce students to the language commonly found in the financial pages of the press. As the students read the headlines, attention should be drawn to the verb and noun forms such as to *gain/a gain*, *to lose/a loss*.

Key:

Good performance: Nos. 3 and 5
Poor performance: Nos. 1, 2 and 4

If possible, bring in an English-language newspaper and read some of the headlines from the financial pages to the class. Introduce some of the less standard forms of *increase* and *decrease* that are used to describe share performance on the Stock Exchange such as *to slide*, *to slip* and *to plummet*.

READING

1 Key:

1 What is another name for 'government stocks'?
2 How much business is done on the Stock Exchange each year?
3 What are three examples of indirect investments on the Stock Exchange?
4 Which companies have recently come onto the stock market?
5 When did the 'Big Bang' happen?

2 Key:

1	Before	4	Before
2	Now	5	Now
3	Now	6	Now

VOCABULARY

1 Key:

1	c	**5**	b
2	c	**6**	b
3	a	**7**	b
4	c	**8**	b

2 The objective of this exercise is for the students to convert the given verbs into the appropriate noun form. After the exercise has been completed, encourage the students to think of other verbs which are converted to nouns using the endings *-ings*, *-ment*, *-tion*, *-ship*.

Key:

1	savings	**4**	partners
2	investments	**5**	quotations
3	competition	**6**	membership

3 Before listening to the recorded passage, the students, working in pairs, should study the different labels carefully and try to identify some of the information featured on the SEAQ screen. They should notice that 'Imp Chem Ind' is an abbreviation for the name of a company and the 'vol 1.2m' corresponds to the volume of trading. After the students have completed as much of the chart as they can, play the passage on tape for the students to find the rest of the information.

Key:

1	e	**5**	f
2	a	**6**	c
3	g	**7**	d
4	b		

Tapescript:

This SEAQ screen shows the prices of Imperial Chemical shares. The name of the company is abbreviated at the top of the screen. At the top right-hand corner of the screen, you can see the figure 630 which is the final price (in pence) of ICI shares at the close of the Stock Exchange yesterday. The second line of the screen, just below the name of the company, shows that 1.2 million ICI shares have already been traded on the Stock Exchange today. Next to this information, the most recent share prices are given. You will notice that these prices are from 631 to 635 pence per share. Since share prices don't change very much from day to day, the last digits only are shown.

Below this, you will notice eight lines of information each containing three different columns. The letters on the left-hand column are abbreviated for market makers, which are member firms of the Stock Exchange. CAZN, for example, is the abbreviation for Cazenove and company, a British securities house. The figures in the middle column are the market makers' quotations. Cazenove, for example, was prepared to buy ICI shares at 632p and sell them at 635p. The right-hand column indicates the quantity of shares in thousands that market makers are prepared to buy and sell at the prices quoted. Finally, in the middle of the screen, we can see a line

of information in enlarged letters on a white background. This gives the names of the market makers offering the best buying and selling prices, which on this day, is 632p for buying and 634p for selling ICI shares.

DISCUSSION

This activity enables students to reflect on a recent development in individual share ownership. Apart from the obvious financial gain involved in share ownership, one of the main advantages for employees of acquiring a stake in their own company is that they can take a greater interest in their jobs and feel more involved in their company. As the work they do daily can, to a certain extent, affect share prices, they are participating directly in the future success of their company. They can hope that the expansion of business will enable their shares to grow in value and provide a dividend each year.

LANGUAGE FOCUS

THIRD CONDITIONAL

Practice

Key:

1 If I had worked as a sales assistant at Fashion World Clothing in 1990, I would have earned £3.60 an hour.
2 If I had changed £100 into Deutschmarks on 23 January 1992, I would have got (received) 286 DM.
3 If I had taken flight LF 903 from Hamburg on 17 October 1992, I would have arrived in Heathrow late.
4 If I had sold my Renault in 1988, I would have got £7,500.
5 If I had bought a compact disc player in 1980, I would have paid £245.
6 If I had owned 100 shares in Marks and Spencer in 1989, I would have received a dividend of £5.60.

SKILLS FOCUS

READING

The purpose of this section is to present the complex information contained in the share price listings found in most newspapers, in relatively simple terms. Nevertheless, it would be useful to read each explanation through with the students, focusing particularly on the listing for Glaxo shares which is highlighted by way of example. Write the four sectors of business that will be featured in the following activity on the board and ask students if they can give an example of one or two British companies in each sector (they may remember ICI from the writing activity in the first unit).

Once the students have understood the explanations, they can begin working in pairs on the share listings taken from 'The Independent'. Go around to each group and provide help when necessary.

Key:

1	**a** 210		**b** 262 1/2		**c** 462
	d 300				

2 Chemical and pharmaceutical:
SKBeechEU (-43), Wellcome (+6)

Food manufacturers:
Nthn Foods/Park Foods (-7), Dalepack (+7)

Oil and gas: Burmah Cstrol (-7), Woodside (+3)

Transport and shipping: Tiphook (-57), Ocean Group (+4)

3 **b** (Kelt Energy). Kelt Energy has lost the most pence
(6.5) and the most value in percentage terms.

4 **a** Highest yield – Fisher J (10.8)

b lowest yield – ManchShip (0.4)

5 **a** 17.5   **b** 14.2   **c** 10.7   **d** 19.9

As a further activity, students at a more advanced level in
business studies should be encouraged to express change in
price as a percentage. If we take the example of Glaxo, we can
say that the share moved 311p between 943p and 632p or
33%. To get this percentage, we divide the difference between
the high and low prices (311) by the high price (943) and
multiply by 100 (33%).

Choose four companies from one of the sectors and ask
students which one showed the greatest percentage change in
price during 1991.

LISTENING I

This short pre-listening exercise focuses on the prepositions
used after expressions of increase and decrease. Illustrate this
point by writing an example on the board: *The average price
of a Paris-London flight in 1990 was £80. In 1992 it was £100.*

In this case, we use a verb of increase or decrease with the
preposition *by*, followed by the appropriate figure: *The
average price of a Paris-London flight increased/rose by £20.*

The same information can be expressed by using a noun form
+ the preposition *of*: *There was an increase/rise of £20 in the
average price of a Paris-London flight.* We can also specify
the highest and lowest figures as follows: *The average price
increased/rose from £80 to £100.*

1 The students should study the table carefully before
deciding which prepositions to use.

Key:

1 by
2 from … to
3 to

*Note: In the third sentence, only the final result of the increase or decrease is
given. This is a common feature of stock market reports.*

4 up
5 of
6 down

*Note: The expressions 'up' and 'down' are also commonly used when
describing increase and decrease in share prices as in sentences 4 and 6.*

7 at

*Note: When there has been no change in share prices, we can use the
expression 'to stand at'.*

2 The students should now be ready to listen to the taped
passage, which should be played as many times as required to
extract the relevant information. The students should be given
about five minutes to make the calculations required for the
'Change +/-' column after which the correct answers can be
given.

Key:

Tapescript:

Trading was relatively heavy on the London Stock
Exchange today. Let's take a look at some of the most actively
traded shares:

Name of share	Yesterday's closing price	Today's closing price	Change (+/-)
Guinness	542p	552p	+10p
Dixons	204p	199p	-5p
Barclays	373p	364p	-9p
South West Water	307p	317p	+10p
Sainsbury	359p	360p	+1p
British Steel	70p	69p	-1p
Rolls Royce	130p	129p	-1p
Boots	423p	424 ½p	+1 ½p
British Aerospace	391p	388p	-3p
National Power	144 ½p	144 ½p	no change

Guinness shares rose from 542p yesterday to 552p. Dixons
fell 5p to 199p. Barclays shares decreased from 373p to 364p.
South West Water increased 10p to 317p and Sainsbury shares
were also up 1p at 360p. British Steel dropped 1p to 69p,
while Rolls Royce shares were also down 1p at 129p. There
was an increase of 1 1/2p in Boots shares which are now at
424 1/2p. British Aerospace fell 3p to 388p while National
Power stood at 144 1/2p.

SPEAKING I AND 2

This activity provides further practice in reading share listings
and enables students to express hypothetical situations in the
past using the third conditional, the grammar point previously
dealt with in the unit. The students should realise that they are
not being asked to choose shares as specialists. However,
depending on recent trends, they will probably be aware of the
fact that certain sectors or companies are in difficulty and
therefore avoid choosing them. It should take the students
about ten minutes to choose their shares and then an additional
five minutes to check the more recent listings found at the
back of the book and work out the profit or loss they would
have made. The students who would have made a particularly
sound (or unwise) investment should be asked to present their
findings to the rest of the class. Make sure that the third
conditional is used correctly.

WRITING

As preparation for this activity, ask the students to bring in a daily newspaper to the lesson. Ensure that you have a selection of newspapers yourself from different days so that every student has access to one.

LISTENING 2

1 After studying the chart, the students will notice that the London Stock Exchange has the highest turnover. This is due to the fact that London is a genuinely international marketplace, as the speaker will mention in the first listening extract.

The extract can be played several times after which the students should be given about five minutes to complete the chart from the notes they have made.

Key:

Stock Exchange	Characteristics
London	– No longer has a trading floor: it now trades on the telephone. – The only genuinely international marketplace in Europe
Frankfurt	– The most important of the 8 German stock exchanges.
Paris	– Relatively small stock exchange. – It is now a continuous market.
Stockholm	– Computers are used to work out how to do business and to decide what the best prices are.

Tapescript:

I think that the important difference that you'll see between London and any other European stock market, or indeed any other stock market in the world, is that London does not any longer have a trading floor where stocks and shares are bought and sold. London has moved from a position where it did trade on the market floor, but now trades on the telephone. All the other exchanges (Paris, Frankfurt, Amsterdam, Copenhagen), all the others, they all still use a trading floor.

They've certainly changed over the years. You shouldn't forget that Frankfurt, for example, is just one German exchange among eight. It's the principal one, but it's not the only exchange, whereas London covers the entire UK. And there the banks are very much a dominant force in the market, so the broking houses and the banks (are) very heavily tied in with one another and they do a lot of business between themselves.

Paris is a relatively small exchange in many ways, but it has taken a lot of steps over the last few years to modernise itself to bring itself up to a standard where it could be a major

stock exchange in terms of its trading hours. For example, it used to only deal for two hours a day, now it's a continuous market.

And the other interesting market for example is Stockholm where there used to be, indeed there still is, what we call a 'call-over' system. The chairman says 'we're now going to deal in Volvo shares' and the brokers standing around used to call out their bids for Volvo shares whether they were buyers or sellers, and how many. Now they do exactly the same thing, except that they all sit at computer terminals and they feed in that information via the computer terminal and the computer works out how best they can do the business, what is the best price.

So the other European exchanges are mainly serving their domestic markets. They're serving their domestic markets. They're serving their domestic customers in terms of companies and they're serving their domestic shareholders. London, by contrast, is trying to be a genuinely international marketplace in Europe.

2 Students are asked to take notes as they listen to the extract. They should then use their notes to help them choose appropriate labels for the graph and pie chart. It would be useful to explain the words *holdings* (used as a synonym for companies in this context) and *wealthy*, as well as the idiomatic expression *in the know*.

Key:

Figure 1: Number of people who own shares in the UK

Figure 2: Number of people involved in the Stock Market in the UK

The extract should be played again so that the students can make a list of the three ways in which people participate in the stock market in the UK.

Key:

1 Share ownership
2 Insurance funds
3 Pension funds

Tapescript:

The answer to how has stock ownership changed is quite simple. Because of the privatisation programme which the present government has undertaken, the number of people who own shares in this country has risen from about 3 million in 1980 to about 11 million in 1990. So there has been much more widespread share ownership in the UK than there had been before. However, that ownership is very lightly spread. The majority of share owners own just one or two holdings, shares in one or two companies, and so it's very thinly spread. That being the case, the attitude to the Stock Exchange over that period has not undergone such fundamental changes. People still think of it as somewhere (where) relatively wealthy people who are 'in the know' actually do business. It isn't of course because with 11 million who are directly involved and an equally large number who are involved through insurance funds that they own, through pension funds that they are beneficiaries of, they are all involved. Probably nine out of ten people are actually involved in the Stock Market. But I have to say, regrettably, that I do believe that it is still regarded as something that other people are involved in rather than ordinary individuals. That is a pity, but I'm afraid that remains a fact, and that's the challenge we've got to face over the next ten years.

Corporate Alliances and Acquisitions

KEY VOCABULARY

The key vocabulary section provides simple definitions of the different types of corporate deals or contracts made in the business world today. However, before the students read through these explanations, introduce the topic by asking questions which should lead the students to produce the vocabulary themselves. The following is a list of questions that could be asked with possible answers.

What options are open to businesses when they are competing with each other in the same market, if they want to avoid a price war? (Co-operate on pricing policies./Form a merger.)

What is one of the most expensive areas of investment (after salaries) in, for example, the automobile or the pharmaceutical industries? (Research and development.)

Can you suggest a way to reduce these high costs? (Form a merger with another company in the same line of business and share R & D costs./Set up a joint venture project to do the R & D for the two companies.)

What advantages can be gained by co-operating with another firm when purchasing raw materials or components? (Bulk buying means lower prices./Economies of scale.)

How have businessmen in the West reacted to the opening up of the East European market? (They have been buying up businesses there/setting up joint ventures.)

Can you think of any examples of companies which have invested there? (For example, Volkswagen's deal with Skoda in the former Czechoslovakia.)

What form did these investments take? (Volkswagen bought a controlling share in Skoda./Acquisition.)

These questions are designed to get students thinking about the present business environment and should lead them into a discussion about co-operation between businesses in general and more specifically about cost sharing in areas such as research and development, and purchasing. Students should also be encouraged to say what they may know about recent acquisitions and joint ventures in Eastern Europe.

LEAD-IN

This exercise provides the students with an opportunity to check that they have fully understood the differences between mergers, joint ventures and acquisitions. Before they start working in pairs, read through the press extracts with the students, explaining any difficult vocabulary such as *the deal was carried off*, and *combined sales*. Check that students are aware that *a subsidiary* is a company where 50% or more of the shares are owned by another company or where another company controls who is on the board of directors.

Key:

1 acquisition
2 merger
3 joint venture
4 joint venture
5 acquisition

READING

As a pre-reading task, ask students what they know about Renault and Volvo. Are the types of car they produce similar?

1 Three comprehension questions precede the text. If the term *economies of scale* has not already been taught, it may be useful to give the translation of this term in the student's native language as opposed to explaining it in English. In this way, when the students come to answer question 1, they will not simply repeat what has been said previously.

Key:

1 Economies of scale are the savings that are gained by operating on a large scale.

2 Renault and Volvo will save money by sharing the costs of product development and research and they will benefit from savings on the purchasing price of components by buying in bulk together.

3 Large businesses can benefit from economies of scale on the production level; the more you produce the cheaper each unit costs to produce.

2 Encourage students to read for specific information and not to be distracted by some of the new but less important vocabulary which features in the article.

Key:

1 Renault
2 Renault
3 Volvo
4 Renault and Volvo
5 Renault
6 Volvo and Renault
7 Volvo

As a further discussion point, ask the students why they feel that Volvo chairman Pehr Gyllenhammar stressed that this was *an alliance*, not a merger or an acquisition.

VOCABULARY

1 Key:

1 capital
2 competitive
3 economies of scale
4 foothold
5 network
6 talks
7 terms
8 effectively

2 Key:

Verb	Noun	Adjective
survive	survival survivor	–
compete	competition competitor	competitive
to profit (from)	profit profitability	profitable
co-operate	co-operation	co-operative
acquire	acquisition	–
negotiate	negotiation negotiator	negotiable

DISCUSSION

An advertisement has been provided as the basis for a discussion. Before reading the advertisement in pairs or small groups, ask the students what they think the advertisement is for. The obvious reaction of the students will be to think that this is a product advertisement for shoes. Check that students understand certain problem words and expressions by writing them on the board and eliciting explanations from the students, for example: *free market* (it would also be interesting to mention *command economy*), *barter* (trade by exchange of goods), *countertrade*, *raw materials* and *seeking to broaden our horizons*.

The pairs or small groups of students should then read the advertisement. Encourage them to discuss their observations. For example, do they think the visual is effective in gaining people's attention? Is the text persuasive in its arguments? Would they have got in touch with Motokov if they were investing in the former Czechoslovakia on the strength of this advertisement? etc. The students should also try to find out why Motokov chose to use a photo of shoes. They will observe the last line of the text: 'no one else is big enough, or skilled enough, to fill our shoes'. Even if a similar expression does not exist in their native language, they could guess what it means. They should also answer the two questions provided for them. When these tasks have been completed they should come together as one big group to discuss their observations and to compare them with those of the other groups.

Key:

1 Motokov is advertising to inform businessmen wishing to invest in the former Czechoslovakia that it is available to provide information and assistance. The advertisement is designed to persuade people to deal with them, by giving information about their background and experience.

2 Motokov could provide vital information about the local market and distribution networks. They could help with all financial negotiations including barter or exchange of goods. They could arrange joint ventures with local

businessmen. They could advise companies looking for new export markets. They could also arrange for the export of goods from Czechoslovakia to various international markets.

LANGUAGE FOCUS

REPORTED SPEECH

Practice

1 **Key:** Refer students to page 157, so that they can check that they have completed the table correctly.

2 Before doing this exercise the students should look very carefully at the language used in the statements. There is a clear indication in each case as to which verb to use, for example, 'It is important – I repeat extremely important' plainly expresses *to stress*. However, there may be some confusion between *to explain* and *to point out* (statements 2 and 8). Either is suitable in both cases.

Key:

1 She stressed that the company should negotiate a joint venture as soon as possible.
2 She explained that joint ventures did not require licences in Hungary.
3 She added that investors enjoyed a five-year tax holiday and could import duty-free.
4 She warned that conditions for doing business would not be ideal.
5 She predicted that this would improve in the next few years.
6 She confirmed that wages were very low in Hungary.
7 She promised that they would keep labour costs to a minimum.
8 She pointed out that the domestic market would soon be saturated.

SKILLS FOCUS

This unit focuses on the skill of describing things and familiarises students with a variety of ways of obtaining and giving information.

LISTENING I

Before listening to the cassette, the students are invited to try and complete the dialogue by studying the table of specifications. As the students read through the table, check that they understand the vocabulary, particularly abbreviations such as *cc* (cubic centimetres) and *b.h.p.* (British horse power) which are used. When completing the conversation which follows, ensure that students are giving complete sentences as answers, such as *Can you tell me something about the engine?* and *What is the maximum speed of this car?* and not simply *the speed?* etc. Correct any consistent errors made by the class as a whole in their suggested answers, after they have presented them all and explain that the ones they will hear on the tape are other possibilities, not necessarily better than the answers they provided themselves. The students can then

listen to the cassette and should complete the table with the words used by the speakers. You should allow as many listenings as necessary for the students to complete the conversation correctly as they will require this language in the activity which follows.

Tapescript and key:

CUSTOMER: Hello, I was wondering if you could tell me the name of this model?

DEALER: Yes, of course. It's the 850i, BMW's top of the range luxury coupé.

CUSTOMER: How powerful is the engine?

DEALER: It has a 300-horsepower V12 engine of about 5,000 cubic centimetres.

CUSTOMER: And how fast does it go?

DEALER: The maximum speed is 248 kilometres per hour and the car can accelerate from 0 to 100 kilometres in 7 seconds.

CUSTOMER: And what is the seating capacity?

DEALER: As you can see, it's a two-door coupé which seats four people.

CUSTOMER: Could you tell me how much petrol it uses?

DEALER: That depends on where you're driving. It consumes 19.8 litres per 100 kilometres in town driving and 8.8 litres per 100 kilometres when driving at 90 kilometres per hour on the open road.

CUSTOMER: And one last question: how much does it sell for?

DEALER: The BMW 850i costs £61,950.

SPEAKING

The students are asked to divide into groups of three. They will have to ask and answer each other questions in order to complete the table. Go around the different groups checking that they are using the structures they have just heard or the correct ones they suggested when completing the table prior to listening. Ensure that students do not simply call out words from the specifications column and that they ask and answer questions using full sentences. Once they have completed the task, invite the students who have cars to give a detailed description of their own car.

WRITING

Before doing this exercise, revise memo writing on page 58 with the students. In their groups they should be encouraged to discuss their choice of car in detail before writing the memo. They should discuss the following in particular: price, petrol consumption, touring conditions and seating capacity. They may have more general reasons for choosing a particular model, for example, style, comfort, or the car which would most impress clients. They should read out their memos and discuss their choice with the other groups. When they have completed this discussion, collect the memos in for correction. This could also be an opportunity to get the students talking about the cars they would like to drive.

LISTENING 2

1 The students will hear Margareta Galfard, Director of Information and Public Affairs for Volvo, France. Point out that the speaker is Swedish and speaks English as a foreign language. Therefore her English, though correct, may sound a little stilted from time to time.

The students are asked to chose the correct alternative (a, b or c) for the different pieces of information about Volvo. They will need to hear the extract more than once.

Key:

1	c	5	b
2	a	6	b
3	b	7	b
4	a		

Tapescript:

My name is Margareta Galfard and I am responsible for Volvo's communication in France where I am Director of Information and Public Affairs. Volvo is a multinational automotive company active in the transport sector, primarily by our cars, trucks and buses; in the marine sector by Volvo Penta who makes marine and industrial engines; in the aerospace sector through Volvo Flugmotor. We are also present though a 50% – nearly 50% – stake in the health and food sector through a company called Procordia and that is along with the Swedish government. Volvo is present in 130 markets all over the world with nearly 70,000 employees. Nearly two years ago Volvo and Renault concluded a very important alliance, as a matter of fact the most important industrial alliance that Volvo ever made. We are, together, today the fourth automotive company in the world and the first truck company in the world and we are, if you compare to other competitors, the leading, together I mean, the leading automotive company in Europe. That means that it is a very, very important alliance.

We also are complementary. That means Volvo, for instance, is very active on the American markets where Renault is not. We are active in Asia, South America, to a small degree in Africa, and of course in Europe, our most important market after the United States. Renault is not present in the United States. But on all the other markets we can help each other because where Volvo is strong Renault is perhaps not that strong and on the contrary, where Renault is very strong, Volvo is not that strong. Take an example: in Asia, Volvo is present since a long time and we have producing facilities. Renault is present but not that strongly, so since the alliance, Renault is helped (between brackets) by Volvo because they can use our marketing organisation, they can use our producing facilities and thus be more present in that important market in the future. On the contrary, Renault will help us on other markets as they do for instance in France.

2 In this listening exercise the students are asked to take notes under three headings. As there is quite a lot of important information given about the Renault-Volvo alliance in these extracts, the students will need to listen to each extract several times, to complete the task. Ensure that students are familiar with the word *component*, which is one of the headings in the exercise, before they listen to the cassette.

Key:

Research and Development
created a company: Advanced Research Partners, one committee for all R & D: joint general research board, committees for car and truck research

Quality
common quality policy, managed by Mr Joucault from Renault for the two companies

Components
agreement concerning sales and distribution of motors and engines, Renault will sell diesel engines to Volvo and Volvo will sell fuel engines to Renault, Renault will sell diesel engines to Mitsubishi through Volvo in Holland

Tapescript:

You can talk about other advantages of this alliance – I can't name them all but I wanted to name some of them. In April 1990 we created a common company called 'Advanced Research Partners' where we decided to find out how the research and development for the two companies should be organised. And there is one common committee for all of the research and development called the 'joint general research board' and there is also one for the car research and one for the truck research.

Quality. Quality is one of the most important things for an automotive industry today. Today we have a common quality manager called Mr Joucault – he is from Renault – and he is responsible for harmonising all the policy, all the strategy, all the work concerning quality for the two partners.

Components are another very, very important part of the alliance. Volvo and Renault have concluded very, very early an agreement concerning the sales and distribution of motors, engines to each other. So Renault will sell diesel engines to Volvo and Volvo will sell fuel engines to Renault. That is a very, very important agreement that we signed in 1991 and this agreement will also be extended to our company in Holland, which is the company where Mitsubishi is active too, and Renault will sell diesel engines to the Mitsubishi cars, so it's a very, very important agreement. These examples are not all the examples of what has been done inside the alliance since the signatures two years ago, but they are sufficiently important to show you that the alliance is a living alliance, that no part of our activity is excluded from the alliance. Everything is concerned by the alliance.

The Small Business

KEY VOCABULARY

Introduce the theme of this unit by asking the class if they have any idea of how to go about setting up a business in their own country. Following this, read through the short description of the four main types of business organisation that are found in the United Kingdom with the students, completing and explaining these definitions where necessary.

Public Limited Companies

As the students have previously studied the unit on the Stock Exchange, they will already know that shares can be traded on the stock market. However, you may wish to check that they have understood that this can only be done by public limited companies. It may be necessary to explain that while both public limited and limited companies have a capital structure that is based on shareholdings, only the shares of the former can be traded on the stock market. While many of the formalities for registering both types of company are the same, the minimum share capital for a public company is much higher.

Sole Trader or Sole Proprietor

Students should realise that as this is the easiest way of setting up a business (no legal formalities, no disclosure of accounts and no business taxation) it is therefore well suited to small-sized operations such as shops.

Partnership

Explain that with this form of business it is almost always necessary to draw up a formal partnership agreement in which the procedures for running the business and the precise role of each partner is defined.

Private Limited Company

Although this is the most common form of business in the UK, students should understand that setting up such a company is no simple matter as it requires specialist advice from a solicitor. Before a limited company can be officially registered, two important documents have to be drawn up: the memorandum of association, and the articles of association.

The first of these documents contains the details concerning the company's share capital and its commercial objectives, and the second lays out rules for the internal management of the company.

When you have read through the definitions, ask the students if they know what the different categories of companies are in their own country. In many cases they will be able to see similarities between the categories used in their country and those of the UK.

LEAD-IN

1 This short section lets students see what information can be deduced from the name of a company. The students will have no difficulty identifying those which are private limited companies (plc) or public limited companies (Ltd) and they will see that the partnership involves two or more individuals and that the sole trader has a single proprietor.

Key:

Public Limited Company – Hoskyns Group plc
Sole Trader – The Tackle Exchange
Partnership – Freed, Stone, Goodman
Private Limited Company – Accolade Europe Ltd.

2 In this section check that the students have fully understood the differences between the three forms that a small business may take and the implications that choosing one of these forms will have on the development and running of a business.

Key:

Advantages		Disadvantages	
1	sole trader	1	partnership
2	partnership	2	partnership/sole trader
3	limited company	3	partnership/sole trader
4	limited company	4	limited company

3 This brainstorming activity is designed to get students to come up with some of the essential questions that need to be considered in the initial stages of preparing a business project. In this way students will be better able to appreciate the difficulties that are faced by entrepreneurs such as Ben Fox, whom they will be reading about in the article 'Deliver us from debt'. The students should first make a list of all the questions that they can find and then discuss them with all the students in one group. A suggested list of questions is given below but there are many others that could be added. It may be helpful to suggest to the students that they group their questions under individual headings, such as finance, organisation, the product, the market.

How much money will I need?

Where will I get this money from?

Is there a market for the product or service that I want to sell?

What competition will there be?

What form of business would be best for me?

What advice will I need?

Where should I locate the business?

How many employees will I need to hire?

LISTENING

In this short extract from an interview with Ben Fox, students should listen for precise information. After playing the passage once, write some of the more difficult words such as *redundant* and *radius* on the board and elicit an explanation from the students to check that they have understood them. When the students have heard the extract sufficiently to complete all the answers, prepare the reading passage that follows by asking questions to see how the students imagine Ben Fox and his company.

Where do you think it is based?
Who are its customers?
What type of a boss do you think he is?

Key:

1 27
2 Fasta Pasta
3 Home delivery service of pasta and sauces
4 May 1990
5 Pizza restaurant company
6 He had been made redundant and he knew that home delivery was potentially a new market

Tapescript:

My name is Ben Fox. I'm 27 years old. I started Fasta Pasta in May 1990. We've just opened our second unit and we operate a home delivery service of fresh pasta and sauces and we deliver to homes and businesses within a mile radius of the shop. I started, having been made redundant about five months previous to when we opened, so about November 1989. But during the end of 1989 there was a lot of information coming out about the popularity of home delivery and that that was potentially a new market in fast food and hence I went down that route of looking into the possibility of setting something up as a home delivery option. I had been involved in, well the company I used to work for was a pizza restaurant company, so I had sort of been involved in fast food to a certain degree.

READING

This article, which is taken from the Financial Times, does present difficulties both in terms of vocabulary, idioms and the use of metaphor and it may be necessary to go over these with the students. A list of these words is provided below. Put this vocabulary on the board and ask students to use their dictionaries to find the meanings of the different words and expressions. The students may need help particularly with some of the more technical terms and idioms.

Metaphors relating to food
gobbled up (line 8)
consumed (line 9)
ladled (line 11)
bear fruit (line 23)
suck up (line 53)

Specific vocabulary
livery (line 14)
rent review (line 56)
hindsight (line 70)
mail drops (line 107)
take-outs (line 90)

Idioms (colloquialisms)
get on one's bike (sub title)
to learn something the hard way (line 3)
to turn up one's nose at something (line 45)

1 In this first reading comprehension exercise students are required to read for gist and to understand what the situation of Fasta Pasta was at the time that this article was written.

Key:

2 Fasta Pasta is going through a difficult time but hopes that with more money it will survive.

2 In this exercise the students are asked to assume the role of Ben Fox at the time when he was considering setting up his business. Bearing in mind that the students have already worked on the preparation of such questions in the Lead-in section, they should be able to find the answers without too much difficulty.

Key:

1 Pasta and sauces for home delivery.
2 Yes, it is increasingly popular.
3 We are the only company to provide such a service.
4 Yes. I have already worked for a pizza restaurant company.
5 I'm looking for a bank loan of around £70,000.
6 I will invest it in machinery and equipment and in renting a property.
7 Yes. I will need more money to open additional outlets. I will obtain this from investors.
8 Through mail drops and by stressing good value, decent service and healthy eating.

VOCABULARY

1 Key:

1 g 2 l 3 j 4 f 5 k 6 d 7 c 8 h 9 e 10 b 11 a 12 i

2 Key:

1	set up	5	premises
2	capital	6	rent
3	branch	7	refurbishing
4	loan	8	lease

DISCUSSION

In this section each pair of students should consider the four quotations and discuss whether they would be prepared to make the same sort of sacrifices themselves. After students have had enough time to think about which of these situations they would be prepared to accept, bring the class together as a whole and ask some of the students to give a sample of their reactions.

LANGUAGE FOCUS
COULD HAVE & PAST PARTICIPLE

Once students have read the explanations for this grammar point, ask them to give examples from their own experience of alternative decisions that they might have taken at certain times in the past. For example: *I could have chosen to study in another school.*

Practice

Key:

Although a key has been provided here, it is obvious that students will produce their variants for the alternatives that were available.

Decision	Alternative
Richard Simpson left his job.	He could have continued to work for Morgan Grenfell.
He decided to buy his own business.	He could have worked for another bank.
He chose to buy Price's.	He could have bought a more modern company.
Shell decided to sell to him.	They could have sold to someone else.
He moved into a prefabricated office.	He could have stayed in his comfortable office.
He took a salary cut of 40%.	He could have kept his old salary.
He brought his father into the business.	He could have taken on a younger executive.
He decided not to sell the subsidiaries.	He could have sold them.

SHOULD HAVE & PAST PARTICIPLE

After students have read the explanations and before getting them to consider the list of examples, draw attention to a recent controversial event or incident from the world of business or the news and make a comment on this in order to illustrate the use of *should have*. Although suggested answers have been given to these example situations, students should be encouraged to concentrate more on the use of *should have*, than be too concerned about getting the 'correct' answer.

For example: *They should have introduced a new model several years ago.*

Practice

Suggested key:

1 They shouldn't have included a ham in the picture. They should have given more thought to cultural differences.

2 They shouldn't have sold the car under such a name in Spain. They should have asked themselves how 'nova' would sound in Spanish.

3 They shouldn't have sold this product in this way in France. They should have included precise written information about the product as part of the packaging.

4 They shouldn't have suggested that the Japanese use rice cookers to prepare the cake mix. They should have researched Japanese attitudes towards food preparation.

5 They shouldn't have sent a woman. They should have understood that in Japan the business world is dominated by masculine values.

6 They shouldn't have targeted only one racial group. They should have marketed the new brand in a different way.

SKILLS FOCUS
LISTENING

1 In this first extract students should read the questions carefully and then give their answers after listening to the passage a second time.

Key:

1 helping to open new units as Development Manager
2 long hours, getting home very late at night
3 pizza was the only option in home delivery
4 in Italy, when he was on holiday
5 because 'fresh pasta' will cook in two to three minutes compared to thirteen for pizza

Tapescript:

When I was working for the pizza restaurant company and helping to open new units, I was quite busy and getting home very late at night and I'm not a wonderful cook. I like to spend my time sort of reading and doing other things and sport and I used to use home delivery quite a lot and basically the only option in home delivery is pizzas and so that's really, that's where it kind of started in terms of, you know, looking at that as an option or as something that isn't, wasn't currently available. And then as I said, when I was on holiday in Italy I came across a takeaway pasta business which kind of sort of made me think a little bit. When I was working for the pizza restaurant company setting up new operations, we were, I was Development Manager for opening a pasta operation alongside the pizza operation and there we were using automated machinery that was well suited to cooking pasta quite quickly. And really pasta is the ultimate fast food, especially fresh pasta which is what we use, because it will cook in two or three minutes as opposed to pizza which will take about thirteen minutes to prepare and cook. That is the sort of basis and then the difficult area is sort of the sauces and that side of things, but basically that your main base product of pasta is relatively, relatively simple and quick to cook.

2 In this extract the students are asked to listen for specific information.

Key:

1 At lunchtime Fasta Pasta delivers mainly to offices and businesses. In the evenings Fasta Pasta's business is residential.
2 The average customer is between 20 and 40. Very many of their customers are women who want a change from pizza and who recognise that pasta is good for them.

Tapescript:

We do quite a lot of lunchtime business in terms of offices and businesses within the area that we deliver. But predominantly it's residential in the evenings and our main client base is I suppose aged between 20 and 40 although we have customers who are over 50 and we have customers who are sort of under 10. The main part of our market is I suppose between 20 and 35, male and female. We're quite surprised by the number of female customers, but I think that's predominantly because they recognise that pasta is good for them and it's a change from pizza as well.

3 In this passage students have to complete the sentences by finding the verbs that Ben Fox uses.

Key:

1	research	4	listen, learn
2	talk	5	get
3	believe		

Tapescript:

To research whatever they want to do very carefully, to talk to friends and relatives and people they know about what they want to do and to really not give up.

You need to believe in what you are doing but you can get a lot of support from people around you and which, which doesn't cost you anything, just costs you some time in talking to people.

To listen to people and to learn from others. And also to get the right sort of background in what you are doing whether it be in terms of working for someone who is doing a similar operation to what you want to do.

SPEAKING

This questionnaire has been adapted from those used by various banks to help their customers to consider whether they have the qualities and personal skills necessary to run a business. Although the vocabulary used in the questionnaire is relatively simple, you may wish to explain the following words and expressions: *to get on with someone, self-starter, to be willing, to cope with, to foresee, reluctantly.*

Make it clear to the students that they should not consider the questionnaire as a test but should answer it as honestly as they can. When they have completed the questionnaire they should discuss their answers with their partner to see how they differ.

Select a sample of students to see what scores they obtained. Ask the students if they feel that the scores they obtained are a true reflection of their own entrepreneurial capacity. As a final stage, ask each pair of students to prepare two further questions that they think should have been included in the questionnaire. These questions should then be circulated around the class.

WRITING

This exercise serves as consolidation for the whole unit while, at the same time, allowing students to use their imagination to find a suitable business project. It may be done either in class with students working in pairs or small groups, or assigned as homework.

International Trade

KEY VOCABULARY

As an introduction to the topic of this unit, ask students if they can name any international trade bodies such as GATT or EFTA. You may also choose to start up a discussion based on any recent trends, such as negotiations, agreements or trade 'wars' between two or more countries. The class should then read through the key vocabulary section.

LEAD-IN

1 The short listening passage featured in this section provides a more in-depth approach to one of the aspects of international trade. Before the students listen to the passage, they should carefully read the three questions that they will be answering. The students will most likely need to listen to the passage several times in order to fully understand the parallel drawn by the speaker between countries and individuals.

Key:

1 He compares countries to individuals.
2 He uses the example of growing one's own food.
3 They should specialise in what they do most efficiently (i.e. where they can make best use of their resources) and buy what they don't produce themselves.

Tapescript:

They trade because it is in their interest to trade. It's the same reason that individuals trade. Individuals are trading all the time. Now, let me give you a kind of example for that, of that. You would not think it was sensible if you spent all your time growing your own food because you would have to work 20 hours a day. You don't have the expertise maybe to do that, you don't have the land to do that or at least it's not good land and therefore it makes more sense to you to do what it is that you do best, OK, and in the process earning enough to buy whatever food you then need. And therefore if individuals are doing what they do best, they are in a position to make best use of their own resources, of their own abilities, of their own talents and they therefore earn more and that allows them to buy what it is they don't produce themselves, and the same logic, exactly the same logic applies to countries.

2 This short 'Europe Quiz' is designed to get students to think about the different geographical, economic and cultural characteristics of the EC countries. Before doing the quiz in pairs, they should first indicate if any countries need to be added to the list of EC members. They should also realise that they will not be penalised for wrong answers. In the key below, actual figures are given in addition to the names of the

countries. This can help to lead the class into an additional discussion about other 'records' held by their countries or about national stereotypes for example.

Find out what made the students come to their decisions and whether they were surprised by some of the 'real' answers.

Key:

1 France (549,000 square km.)
2 Germany (61.5 million inhabitants)
3 Ireland (16.6%)
4 Netherlands (439 inhabitants per square km.)
5 Germany (approximately 16.5% of France's total exports goes to Germany)
6 Benelux countries (approximately 18.9% of Germany's total exports goes to the Benelux countries)
7 Germany (approximately 5.9% of America's total exports goes to Germany)
8   a United Kingdom
    b France
    c Germany
    d Spain
9   a France (1,255 million tonnes per year)
    b United Kingdom (42.1 kg. per inhabitant per year)
    c Italy (79 litres per inhabitant per year)
    d Greece (2,947 cigarettes per inhabitant per year)
10 a Luxembourg (5 million tonnes)
    b Spain (26 kg. per inhabitant)
    c Ireland (6 litres per inhabitant)
    d Netherlands (1,044 cigarettes per inhabitant)
11 France (approximately 76% of France's electricity is produced in nuclear plants)
12 Germany (6,908 magazines in circulation)
13 Denmark (44.9% of the workforce compared tp 30.3% in Spain)
14 Netherlands (36 1/2 days per year, compared to 22 days in Portugal and Greece)
15 Netherlands: Royal Dutch Petroleum was the top EC company in 1992, followed by British Petroleum (UK), Daimler-Benz (Germany), Fiat (Italy), Shell Transport and Trading (UK), Volkswagen (Germany), Siemens (Germany), VEBA (Germany), Elf Aquitaine (France), Philips Electronics (Netherlands)

READING

This text features an insider's description of the problems involved in importing and exporting between Spain and the UK. Ask the students to read out the import value chart, to ensure they are reading the figures correctly. Several expressions such as *single-handedly*, *bumper crops*, *fully-fledged* and *with the advent of* may have to be reviewed, but the importance of reading for global comprehension should be stressed.

Key:

1 c 2 b 3 b 4 c 5 a

VOCABULARY

In pairs, the students are required to use vocabulary from the reading text in order to complete this crossword. Encourage students to check any unfamiliar vocabulary in an English-English dictionary.

Key:

Across
1 trade
3 goes down
8 member
10 market
11 his
12 guidelines
14 met
16 quotas
18 fax
19 labour
22 joint
24 UK
26 liaison
27 entry
28 duty
29 free
30 trial

Down
2 demand
4 desk
5 worth
6 regulation
7 buys
9 rights
10 ministry
13 staff
15 treaty
17 exporter
20 advice
21 sole
23 and
25 key

THE INVOICE

The purpose of this task is to introduce students to one of the documents commonly used in the context of international trade. In the case of students who are following a core curriculum in international trade, it may be useful to point out some of the other types of documents and their purpose as these often come up on examination papers.

The *bill of exchange*: an unconditional order in writing sent and signed by one person (*the drawer*) to another (*the drawee*) requiring the drawee to pay on demand or at a future time a sum of money to or to the order of a specified person (*the payee*).

The *bill of lading*: a receipt given by the shipping company upon shipment of goods. It is a document of title and is thus required by the importer to clear the goods at the point of destination.

The students should first study the information contained in the model invoice and ask questions if they are unfamiliar with certain terms (*issue*, *freight* or *warehouse*, for instance). The recorded passage should then be played, more than once if necessary.

Key:

1	7th May 1992	7	£390
2	699	8	£60
3	160	9	£14,450
4	120	10	16
5	40	11	10
6	£14,000	12	BRX 43 1992

Tapescript:

By looking at the invoice number 699, you will notice that on 7th May 1992, the Metropolitan Tennis Equipment Company of Los Angeles shipped a total of 160 tennis rackets to Champion Sport Ltd. in London. The shipment included 120 of the 'GX12' model priced at £78 and 40 of the 'Tennis Pro' model at £116, for a total of £14,000. The cost of freight was £390 and the insurance from warehouse to warehouse was £60. The total amount to be paid by the UK importer was hence £14,450. The rackets were packed in 16 cardboard cartons, 10 per carton, on which the words MET CS LTD. LONDON 1-16 were written. The import licence number was BRX 43 1992. The invoice was signed by an official of the exporting company, Mr Robert Morales.

LANGUAGE FOCUS

MODAL VERBS: OBLIGATION

If the students are not sure which verbs express obligation, necessity or advice, provide help by giving simple examples, such as *You should go to the cinema more often*, or *You don't have to call the bank to order a new cheque book. It is done automatically.*

Key:

obligation or necessity	have to – must/mustn't – need to
mild obligation or advice	should/shouldn't – ought to
absence of obligation or necessity	don't have to – needn't – don't need to

Practice

1 There are several answers in each case. The students should be encouraged to come up with as many as possible.

Suggested answers:

1 You should arrange appointments with German buyers in advance.
2 You needn't present a big collection, but it should have character.
3 The quality of your product must be high.

4 You have to respect delivery deadlines.
5 You don't have to pay by letter of credit.
6 You must type out all prices in foreign currencies and convert them into Deutschmarks.
7 You should employ an agent to help you deal with German companies.

2 Students are required to draw up a short guide giving advice to an American delegation who will be visiting their country.

DESCRIBING TRENDS

Practice

1 Key:

Adverbial forms:
steadily (draw attention to the change from *y* to *i*)
gradually
slightly
sharply
dramatically (draw attention to the spelling change)
suddenly

2 Before beginning this exercise, ask students to identify the different types of graph shown i.e. *a bar chart* and *a line graph*.

Key:

1 steadily/gradually
2 sharply/dramatically/suddenly
3 slightly
4 steady/gradual
5 sharp/sudden/dramatic
6 slight

3 Students should be asked to study the graph so that they can 'visualize' the new expressions being introduced. Although they may know the words *fluctuate* and *stable*, provide short explanations for each of the following expressions, and illustrate them with curves drawn on the board:

to fluctuate	to rise and fall irregularly
to reach a peak	to reach the highest point
to level off	to reach stability after a period of movement
to stand at	to be at certain point at a given time
to remain stable	to show no change

The students should now do the matching exercise based on the graph.

Key:

1c **2**e **3**b **4**a **5**d

SKILLS FOCUS

WRITING

Before doing the graph interpretation exercises which follow from this point on, it may be useful to review quickly the prepositions used after expressions of increase and decrease, either by having students refer to the 'Stock Exchange' unit or by dictating or writing the following examples on the board, leaving out the prepositions in order to create a short gap-filling exercise.

There was a rise/increase *of* 3% in the unemployment rate between 1985 and 1992.

The number of shares traded on the stock exchange rose/increased *by* 15 million between November and December 1989.

From . . . to is used to specify the initial and final positions in a set of statistics:

The number of people employed in the UK shipbuilding industry decreased/fell *from* 25,000 *to* 8,000 between 1982 and 1987.

It is important to draw attention to the fact that in each of the examples given above, the simple past is the only verb tense used because in each case, past trends are being described.

The students should then write a short interpretation of the graph either individually or in pairs. Make sure that the vocabulary from the previous activities is being used to describe the different trends (*to decrease steadily, to reach a peak, to level off*, etc.).

LISTENING I

1 The recorded passage should be played several times so that the students can fill in all the blanks in the description of the graph.

Key:

1	stood at	**5**	reaching a peak
2	rose slightly	**6**	fluctuated
3	sharply	**7**	climbing to
4	dramatic	**8**	levelled off

Tapescript:

In 1965, the price of New Zealand wool stood at $1.98 per kilo. It then rose slightly by 20 cents in 1966 before falling sharply to $1.37 in 1971. There was a dramatic increase over the next two years, with the price of wool reaching a peak of $5.13 in 1973. From 1974 to 1978 the price fluctuated between a high of $3.20 and a low of $2.75, before climbing to $4.60 in 1980. After falling again to $3.60 in 1983, the price levelled off at $3.55 in 1985.

After the missing words have been filled in, the students should be asked to point out the sections of the graph which posed a problem. The students will have noticed that there are different ways of interpreting a graph and should be encouraged to use these in the next series of activities.

2 Several sections of the three graphs have been deleted. The students must listen to the cassette in order to complete them. As they listen they should plot the data on the graphs. The passages should be played as often as necessary for them to finalise their answers.

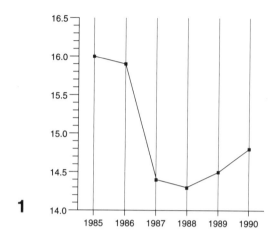

1 Production of Coal – Spain
1985-1990 (in millions of metric tons)

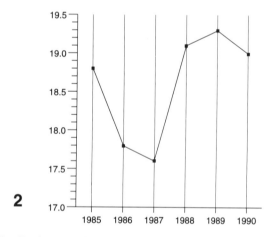

2 Production of Crude Steel – France
1985-1990 (in millions of metric tons)

Tapescript:

GRAPH 1: Production of Coal – Spain

By looking at the first graph, you will notice that from 1985 to 1986 the production of coal remained stable: in 1985, 16 million tonnes of coal were produced and this figure decreased only slightly to 15.9 million tonnes in 1986. In 1987, the amount of coal produced by Spain dropped sharply by 1 1/2 million tonnes and continued to decrease to 14.3 million tonnes in 1988. After a slight increase to 14.5 million tonnes in 1989, the amount of coal produced rose again and levelled off at 14.8 million tonnes in 1990.

GRAPH 2: Production of Crude Steel – France

On the second graph, which represents France's production of crude steel, we can see the following trends over the six-year

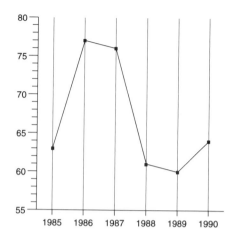

3 Production of Wine – Italy
1985-1990 (in millions of hectolitres)

period. In 1985, France produced 18.8 million tonnes of crude steel. The total production fell by 1 million tonnes in 1986. After a slight drop to 17.6 million tonnes in 1987, production increased dramatically over the next two years. Indeed, in 1988, the figure rose to 19.1 million tonnes and in 1989, production of crude steel reached a peak of 19.3 million tonnes. This was followed by a decrease of 300,000 tonnes in 1990.

GRAPH 3: Production of Wine – Italy

The third graph shows the production of Italian wine. You will notice that the amount of wine produced stood at 63 million hectolitres in 1985 and then rose sharply to reach a peak of 77 million hectolitres in 1986. The following year there was a slight decrease of 1 million hectolitres before a sudden drop of 15 million hectolitres in 1988. The amount of wine produced fell slightly to 60 million hectolitres in 1989 and then finally levelled off at 64 million hectolitres in 1990.

SPEAKING

1 The purpose of this activity is to have students exchange information interactively. Divide the class into groups of four and assign a different graph to each student. The students should first study the information on their graphs individually and then take turns describing it to the other members of the group. As each student gives his/her commentary, the other members of the group should plot this information on their graphs using the symbols provided. Go around each group making sure that the information is being presented with the language structures studied previously and that the figures are not being simply read (i.e. *24 million tonnes in 1986, 27 million tonnes in 1987*, etc.).

2 Once each student has completed his or her presentation, the group can now answer the seven questions given in their books. If the students give different answers, it may be because their graphs were not drawn correctly in the previous phase. The students should then compare their graphs to identify where the error was made.

Key:

- USA
- EC
- 14 million tonnes
- 1988 (total of 95 million tonnes)
- EC and Australia both exported 15 million tonnes in 1987
- 1989 and 1990
- Australia

LISTENING 2

1 This first listening extract examines the concept of 'protectionism' which was dealt with briefly in the Key Vocabulary section and which probably came up in the discussion which followed. The students should focus on the arguments put forward by the speaker and decide whether the statements are true or false. You may wish to give synonyms for some words and expressions used, for example: *to restrict* (synonym: 'to limit'), *interest groups* (synonym: 'lobbies', which is probably more familiar), *clout* (synonym: 'power'), etc.

Key:

1 True	**4** False
2 False	**5** False
3 True	

Tapescript:

Now the problem with protectionism is that countries often believe it to be in their interest to restrict trade and by that, that usually means restricting imports into their economies. Why do they do this? Well, it often comes from pressure from interest groups within countries who see themselves threatened by imports from another country and they have the type of organisation or the type of power, clout if you like, to influence government decisions in order to bring about some form of, some type of protection to restrict imports. The argument for restricting imports is one that is superficially attractive because it seems to mean protecting jobs and helping to prevent unemployment, which everyone recognises as a serious problem.

But it is only superficially attractive and in fact is fundamentally flawed, because it is the type of argument that actually leads to more unemployment in the future, because it is actually encouraging people to be inefficient and not to use their own talents and abilities and resources to the best ability. If the Japanese make cars more cheaply than another country, for example the US, it is in the US, in the interest of the United States, also to allow those imports of Japanese cars and to divert the US's resources to making something which it makes itself better than it makes motor cars.

2 The second listening extract deals with the various effects of the European Community's Common Agricultural Policy (CAP). The students should take notes using the headings provided as a guide. The words *to fetch*, *a gap* and *corrective* may need to be reviewed.

Key:

EC farmers and producers	CAP helps to give them a higher level of income
EC food prices	CAP maintains EC prices higher than world prices
EEC production	CAP increases production, but tends to generate surpluses. Exports have to be subsidised
EC's trading partners	have reacted strongly against the CAP which they see as an aggressive policy

Tapescript:

The CAP, well that of course stands for the Common Agricultural Policy of the European Community and it is essentially a system of protecting European agriculture in the interest of European farmers and to some extent in the interest of European consumers – at least that is as the objectives of agricultural policy in the Community have been set out. Now, the basic idea is to favour Community producers over other producers (this is the idea of 'community preference') and the idea is to maintain a level of income in fact, for European farmers which is probably considerably higher that it would be in the absence of this Common Agricultural Policy. This is done by a series of mechanisms which help to maintain internal prices in the EC higher than world prices or higher than the prices indeed would be in the absence of these measures. Now, the one consequence of this is to encourage production. Indeed that was part of the objective of the policy, and in a sense it has been over-successful in that it has tended to generate surpluses. Now, surpluses are not necessarily a bad thing because that is what one usually exports. However in this particular case, in the case of the CAP, if you have been generating these surpluses at prices above what they would fetch at world markets, you can only export them if you use export subsidies, basically to close the gap between the domestic price and the price you can get on the world market. And this has created a lot of difficulties in international trade with the EC's trading partners. It has led to what some have described as a 'trade war', because other countries have adopted other similar, sometimes not so similar, but at least corrective policies to oppose what they see as EC aggression in trade.

Insurance

KEY VOCABULARY

This section introduces students to the basic terminology of insurance and explains how companies and individuals can protect themselves by taking out insurance to cover the risks that they are exposed to. It is important that students should fully understand the key concepts that are illustrated here as these form the basis of much of the work that they will be doing throughout this chapter. Before going over the key vocabulary itself ask the students to produce examples of insurance that they or their relatives have taken out and to explain what risks they think these policies cover.

LEAD-IN

These six short listening extracts provide examples of some of the more common risks that are insured against both by private individuals and by businesses. The students will have no difficulty identifying the majority of these but they may, however, need some assistance in distinguishing between the terms *burglary* and *theft*. The former refers to the crime of entering a building with the intention of stealing something while the latter is the term for actually stealing someone's private property.

Key:

1	third party	4	theft
2	burglary	5	fire
3	personal injury	6	breakage

Tapescript:

Speaker 1: In a business like this where basically you're transporting people from one place to another, there's always a danger that a passenger may fall and injure himself or, for that matter, that one of our vehicles might accidentally damage someone else's property.

Speaker 2: Well soon after we moved into this neighbourhood we noticed that just about all the houses in the street were equipped with alarm systems and that several had already been broken into.

Speaker 3: In my career as a professional model I spend a lot of time in front of the cameras being photographed both in studios and at fashion shows. You can't do this sort of job unless your body is in good shape, not just because you have to look your best at all times but also because you're constantly on the move.

Speaker 4: Our museum has some very valuable paintings in its major collections and although we have spent a lot of money on security systems there's still a remote chance that someone might be able to steal one.

Speaker 5: There are quite a lot of potential dangers in running any restaurant business but in my case I think the main worries are that we are using electrical appliances and gas stoves to prepare and cook food, often at very high temperatures.

Speaker 6: In any retail business you want the customer to see what you are selling and, of course, having a large area of window display is one of the best ways to do that.

READING

This passage gives a simple description of how the insurance business is organised in the United Kingdom. While the text itself presents no major difficulties, it may be useful to draw attention to the following vocabulary:

made up of	(line 1)
reinsurance	(line 5)
on behalf of	(line 33)
wine taster's palate	(line 38)
accredited	(line 51)

The term *reinsurance* refers to the way in which the insurance companies spread a percentage of the risks that they have underwritten by reinsuring these with a specialised reinsurance company. For example, a small insurance company or a Lloyd's syndicate might accept a large risk for which it would be unable to provide compensation in the event of a total loss. It would therefore have to reinsure a part of this risk.

1 Key:

	Insurance companies	Lloyds of London	Insurance Brokers
1	✓	✓	–
2	✓	–	–
3	✓	–	–
4	–	–	✓
5	–	✓	–
6	–	✓	–
7	–	–	✓
8	✓	✓	–

2 Key:

1	False	4	False
2	True	5	False
3	True		

3 Key:

1	aviation	4	travel
2	motor	5	marine
3	marine/fire/accident		

VOCABULARY

1 Key:

1 brokers **2** names or members **3** clients

2 Key:

1 i **2** e **3** b **4** f **5** a **6** h **7** d **8** c **9** g

3 Key:

1 member/name
2 syndicate
3 cover/risks/policies
4 underwrite
5 premiums
6 claims
7 compensation

DISCUSSION

This section provides students with a selection of some of the risks that have been insured at Lloyd's of London. Numbers 3, 4 and 5 are examples of how insurance can be used as a means of generating publicity since the items insured have no intrinsic value. However, in the other cases students will need to give serious consideration to the risks involved. Ask students to work on these cases either in pairs or in small groups. While doing so, students should be encouraged to use the modals *may*, *might* and *could* to express the risks that are present in each case. Once the class has had sufficient time to prepare, select sample answers from different pairs (groups) and ask the class if they agree with these conclusions. When the students have expressed their views, present the details of the insurance that was actually underwritten at Lloyd's using the information provided below.

1 All of these singers were insuring against one or more of a variety of risks including loss of their personal possessions, damage to highly valuable equipment, cancellation of concerts and losing their voices. Bruce Springsteen, for example, has insured his voice for £3.5 million.

2 The pictures on display at the Van Gogh exhibition were insured for £3 billion against loss and damage.

3 The cigar was insured against loss when it was displayed at a London exhibition. Although it was insured for its retail value of £17,933, the premium that had to be paid was only 50p.

4 Cutty Sark protected itself against someone winning the prize and actually capturing the monster by taking out a Lloyd's policy to cover this risk. The value of the insurance cover was equivalent to the value of the prize.

5 The forty members of the 'Whiskers Club' each insured their beards for £20 against fire and theft.

6 The organisers of the festival arranged for insurance against bad weather. The policy provided cover for up to £1 million of claims if rain forced the cancellation of any of the 42 performances.

LANGUAGE FOCUS

EXPRESSING APPROXIMATION

Other examples:

approximately (para 8)
approximately (para 10)

Practice

Explain to the students that they will need to round off the figures in the table in order to make them into approximations. They should then comment on at least four of the items presented in the table. Several examples of the types of comments that they might make are given below.

- Nearly 26,000 employees work in the UK.
- They have some 8.5 million customers.
- They have about £50 billion funds under their management.
- In 1991 they made roughly £250 million profits before tax.
- Prudential Corporation's premium income from long term business was around £6 billion in 1991.

SKILLS FOCUS

LISTENING

1 This first listening exercise serves to develop the information about Lloyd's that was presented in the reading passage and to define more precisely the roles of the four main groups of people who are involved in the Lloyd's market. Play this extract several times, then check to see how much information the students have been able to find.

Key:

Syndicates
There are 350 of these and each one operates as a small insurance company which usually specialises in one particular type of insurance.

Underwriters
They represent a syndicate and take responsibility for underwriting insurance risks on behalf of its members.

Lloyd's Brokers
They offer insurance risks to the underwriters. They must be approved by a Lloyd's committee. They bring business onto the Lloyd's market.

Names
They provide the financial backing for a syndicate. To become a member you must have £250,000 in free assets (capital which can easily be converted into cash should the syndicate make a loss).

Lloyd's is one of the oldest established organisations in the British market and it comprises effectively some 350 separate underwriting syndicates which operate as small insurance companies, each syndicate has its own specialisation and a reputation in that particular market. The syndicate in turn comprises an underwriter who actually sits in a little box in the Lloyd's building and he actually underwrites and takes on the risk that is being offered to him by the broker but the finance comes from, anything between, say, 100 and 300 individuals who are underwriting members of Lloyd's or known as 'names'. Now to become a 'name' at Lloyd's you have to establish a certain degree of wealth. When I became a member you had to have at least £75,000 of free assets, it is now £250,000 and perhaps that is not enough. And it is the aggregate of those assets that enables the underwriter to take on risks. When you become a member of Lloyd's you appear before a thing called the Rota Committee and it is made quite clear to you then that the whole of your wealth is committed to this operation. It is what is known as unlimited liability . . . All business comes to Lloyd's direct from Lloyd's brokers who have to be approved by the committee of Lloyd's as people of the right standing, of integrity and professionalism.

2 In this extract the students have to listen for specific information in order to answer two questions. They should be able to identify the three advantages after listening to the cassette once. They can then listen again to find the underlying explanations and a third time to complete the vocabulary exercise. Point out that the speaker in fact mentions 'reputation' as both the first and the third advantage. However, in the first case he is referring to Lloyd's historical reputation for paying claims whereas in the second case he is talking about Lloyd's reputation in marine insurance and about its network of agents.

Key:

1   reputation, low operating expenses, international reputation as a marine insurer

2   –   Lloyd's has never failed to pay claims and it was the only insurer to pay up quickly after the San Francisco earthquake of 1906.
    –   Lloyd's does not have a branch organisation
    –   Lloyd's agents are present throughout the world.
    –   Lloyd's is recognised as the authority on marine insurance

3 a   strengths
    b   failed
    c   operating expenses
    d   cutting out
    e   keep down
    f   in the field of
    g   authorities

Tapescript:

Yes certainly. I think the first advantage is its reputation. This is one of Lloyd's great strengths in that it has never failed to pay a claim in the whole of its history and it made its reputation in the Great San Francisco Earthquake of 1906, when Lloyd's alone amongst all the insurance companies, both British and American, paid up without demur and extremely quickly and that reputation lasts to this day.

The second advantage traditionally is that its operating expenses are rather less than the insurance companies in that it does not have a branch organisation throughout the country because branches are very expensive to maintain.

That direct access, cutting out the branch organisation enables us to keep down costs, and perhaps the third advantage that Lloyd's has is its international reputation. It has a system of Lloyd's agents that operate throughout the world and particularly in the field of marine insurance you will find that Lloyd's really are the leaders, they are the authorities traditionally and still to this day.

3 In this extract students are asked to listen for the key words that the speaker uses when talking about three aspects of Lloyd's. Once the students have identified these words, ask the class to explain the nature of the changes that they refer to.

In the last part of this exercise the students have to pay particular attention to the exact words and the tenses that the speaker uses in order to identify which changes are planned and which are already happening.

Key:

1   a   limiting losses, limited
    b   increasing, overwrite
    c   accessible, establishing representation, presence

2   Don Raley thinks changes are necessary as a result of the very bad results of recent years.

3   Liability: planned (. . . there are various ideas)

    Regulation: already happening (. . . there is increasing regulation)

    Marketing: already happening (. . . are establishing representation)

Tapescript:

Yes, of course, it must change. The system of operation I think will change in that in common with the whole insurance industry, we've had some very bad results in recent years and that has been extremely painful to some of the names, like myself, who have been on syndicates that have had very substantial losses and there are various ideas of limiting losses and introducing a form of limited liability.

Furthermore there is increasing regulation of both the brokers and the underwriters to ensure that they do not, what is known as 'overwrite', write more insurance than they are capable of covering, and from a marketing point of view Lloyd's must be made more accessible to the general public. That is beginning to happen now in that a number of Lloyd's brokers and even some of the Lloyd's syndicates are establishing representation in the towns not to the same extent as the insurance companies with their branches but there is at least a Lloyd's presence there.

SPEAKING

As this activity is quite complex, full explanations have been provided to show students both how insurance companies define a 'standard driver' and also how the type of car will affect the level of the premium that is paid. Before starting the activity, conduct an informal discussion using the information that students have already provided about their own or their relatives' insurance cover in the Lead-in section in order to illustrate how premiums vary according to the profile of the driver and the model of the car. Before the students go on to read the introduction to the activity, elicit or pre-teach the following vocabulary: *convictions, suspension of licence, infirmity, heart condition, spare parts, no-claims bonus* and *to collide*.

The students should be given ample time to consider all the information concerning the three people who are applying for insurance. It may be useful to suggest to them that they should first make a list of the criteria that they will use in their evaluations (age, health, driving record etc.). They can then award plus or minus points to each applicant, based on the information that is given in the application forms. As they are doing this, go round the class to answer any questions that may arise and to help any groups who may find it difficult to come to a decision.

WRITING

Once students have completed the discussion phase of the activity, their conclusions should be presented in a short report assigned for homework. This report should explain which of the applications they would accept and under what conditions (higher premium imposed, requests for additional information, special clauses etc.). Collect these reports and subsequently circulate a number of them around the class to show the students some of the conclusions that were reached. Following this, give a brief explanation of how these applications would have been evaluated by a professional insurer. A summary of this is provided below.

1   Zaniewski. This driver's profile has some questionable features. For instance, he has no permanent address, has no checkable insurance history prior to 1991 and has been resident in the UK for less than three years. Furthermore his profession, although not specifically included in the list of prescribed occupations, is not a standard one. Also, his involvement in an accident with a motorcycle and subsequent conviction in 1991 would give cause for concern. He therefore does not represent an attractive risk and more information would be required before offering him insurance cover. If Zaniewski provides adequate explanations especially concerning his infirmity and his future domicile he would qualify for insurance but on condition that driving be limited to acceptable, named persons. In any case the premium that he would pay would be higher than normal.

2   Brown. The Golf GTi is a 'hot' car which is attractive both to young drivers and also a target for car thieves. This proposal has all the signs of a young person's car being insured in the name of a parent in order to obtain more favourable conditions. Before accepting this risk, the underwriter will first have to establish who is the owner and main driver of the vehicle. Unless J Brown is excluded from the policy, this risk will be rated as that of a young driver. This risk should be restricted to third party cover. However, if certain precautions are taken such as limiting driving to named persons and possibly excluding theft cover, comprehensive cover could be arranged but only at a much higher premium than normal.

3   Campbell. This driver has impaired sight but his motor insurance record is excellent as shown by his no-claims bonus. It appears that he has adjusted to his disability and most underwriters would accept him at normal terms. Emma Brown has had two minor accidents and this means that special accidental damage conditions may have to be applied when she is in charge of the car.

Corporate Identity

KEY VOCABULARY

Introduce the concept of corporate identity by giving examples of companies which have a very strong corporate or brand image, such as IBM and Benetton, and by asking the students what opinions or attitudes they have towards them. Later, in the Lead-in section, the students will be asked to consider how and why their opinions have been formed. The Key Vocabulary section introduces the fact that many aspects of the company contribute to projecting a particular image to various publics and explains who those publics are.

LEAD-IN

1 In this section the students are asked to study in more detail the contributing factors that make up the corporate identity. They are asked to think about the identity of two well-known companies in their countries. Good examples to study are: the national airline company, the telecommunications or transport companies (usually state-owned), or a fashion manufacturer whose products are well known to the students.

2 In the unit on advertising and marketing the students studied in detail product advertising. They are now given an opportunity to analyse a corporate advertisement. The questions are designed to get students thinking about how the advertisement was devised and how the central message is communicated.

For example, in question 1 the students examine the advertisement for information about the company and they learn that BP, a world-famous petroleum company, supplies solar energy equipment to remote parts of the world.

– Question 2 is designed to illustrate that this kind of advertisement generates positive feelings towards the company.

– In Question 3 the students are asked to study in more detail the language used and to see the importance of working in this type of advertisement. For example, the first words are: *Thanks to BP*. Other positive words include *future*, *brighter*, *power*, *children* and *sun*, and the reader automatically associates these words and images with BP.

– Possible answers to Question 4 include: The company is trying to project a caring, responsible and forward-looking image, all of which is summed up in their slogan 'for all our tomorrows'.

When each of the pairs has finished discussing the questions, they should present their findings to the class.

READING

Introduce this task by examining the importance of the logo as part of corporate identity in general. One way of doing this is to bring in a selection of logos, to see how many of these the students can identify. It is also interesting to point out that BP considers its logo to be one of its most important assets.

1 Key:

A 5 **B** 1 **C** 4 **D** 2 **E** 3

2 Key:

1 BP felt that they needed to change their identity because the structure of the group had changed significantly (with the acquisition of new companies and the establishment of separate businesses).

2 It instructed them to examine the effect that recent changes had had on BP's staff and the general public.

3 It showed that the staff wanted BP to be more 'dynamic, innovative, international and better related to the customer' while at the same time being perceived as 'a good employer and socially responsible'.

4 The results established that the public felt that the company should use technology with the future in mind while showing concern for the society and the environment.

5 The group came to the conclusion that BP needed to create a new style, while at the same time retaining the BP shield.

6 David Walton says that image is important 'because it signals commitment and purpose, commands respect and gives competitive advantage'.

VOCABULARY

1 Key:

1 c 2 i 3 g 4 d 5 j 6 h 7 e 8 f 9 a 10 b

2 Key:

1	competitive advantage	5	stand for
2	carry out	6	commitment
3	perception	7	impact
4	poll		

3 Key:

1	international	5	cohesive
2	dynamic	6	responsible
3	professional	7	distinctive
4	innovative		

DISCUSSION

In this section the students are asked to comment on some BP advertisements from the past. These advertisements portray a very different image from the one the students studied in the Lead-in section. In 1935 BP were selling a product that only the wealthy could afford, therefore the advertisement bearing the slogan 'for snappy engines' reflects the lifestyle that car owners had at that time. BP 'controls horse power' is designed to give the company a competent and powerful image, whereas 'buy from the BP pump' features the expert (a man in a suit and tie) advocating the reliability and quality of BP's products. The corporate advertisement seen in the Lead-in section shows BP as a company concerned about people and the environment, two considerations which appeal to BP's customers today.

LANGUAGE FOCUS

THE ARTICLE

Refer students to the Language Focus section at the back of the book where the rules for the article are given in more detail, if students are having problems with this point.

Key:

sunlight (no article)	home (no article)
the energy	*the* sun
electricity (no article)	*the* children
a village	*the* world

- *Sunlight* and *electricity* are used in their general sense and therefore do not take an article.
- the expression *at home* never takes an article.
- *Children* takes the definite article because a specific group of children is being defined, i.e. those on the African continent.
- *Energy* also takes the definite article because it refers to the specific amount of energy that Colin requires to finish his homework.
- *Village* takes the indefinite article as the term is being introduced and no information is given to differentiate this 'remote African village' from other similar villages.
- *Sun* and *world* invariably take the definite article when referring to these unique elements of the universe.

Practice

1 As an introduction to this practice exercise, ask the students what they know about the mineral water company Perrier. To guide the students, ask specific questions like: *What image does the product have? What image crisis did they have to face recently?*

When the students have completed the gap-filling exercise and presented their answers, conclude by asking the students (a) how Perrier dealt with the problem and (b) what the students think of this solution.

Key:

1 the
2 a
3 The
4 A
5 the
6 a
7 a
8 a
9 a
10 An
11 an
12 the
13 The
14 no article
15 no article
16 no article or 'the' are both possible here, depending on whether the term 'consumers' is considered to refer to a specific group (Perrier consumers) or is being used in its wider sense (consumers in general).

Note: Benzene is a substance obtained from coal tar, often used as a solvent.

SKILLS FOCUS

LISTENING

Before beginning this exercise, lead in by discussing with students what they think a design consultancy might do. Play the extract as many times as is required for students to complete the table.

1 Key:

1	tired and dated	5	management
2	diversify	6	staff
3	famous and recognised	7	suppliers
4	who the target market is		

Tapescript:

There are basically two areas that we would be involved in. One would be what we call a 'tweak' of an existing identity and it might be that a company has an identity that is tired, dated, maybe slight irrelevant to the product that it is now in. As I said previously, if a company is going to diversify and certainly in this climate a lot of companies are, the logo that they previously had maybe very relevant to that particular area of business but no longer is … is completely relevant to the new business ventures that they wish to go into. The other area that we get heavily involved in, is completely create a new identity for a brand new company for something that doesn't exist and where it has to become quite famous and recognised in a very short space of time. The company depends on building up its image through the identity both internally and externally and of course in that particular instance we have to do a very in-depth research into what that company wants to be, who the target market is, and at the end of the day who they're going to sell their products to. So with that, it is a matter of creating an image that fulfils a very strong strategic brief. Now, we would work very closely with the management of that company and help create the brief for the new corporate identity design, we would interview the staff, we would talk to the people, we'd talk to the customers and the suppliers of that company, and really find out exactly what it is that makes that company tick and what the benefit of that company is against the competitors.

2 Before listening to the cassette the students should discuss how the logos have changed and give their opinions of the new logos. Once the students have filled in the table they may wish to discuss the solutions proposed by Michael Peters Ltd. and say whether they like them or not. The students may have other solutions to put forward and these too can be discussed.

Key:

	Problem of old identity	Solution
BBC	The public felt that it was not up to date with the latest technology and seemed indifferent to local needs.	Redesigned the logo and introduced a colour-coded system to give a local image to each channel.
ATS	People assumed that they only offered a tyre service.	Changed the name from Associated Tyre Specialists to ATS and introduced a set of visual images to illustrate the other areas of business.

Tapescript:

The first one, the BBC, was basically a re-design of what they had. They already had what they call the boxes, the three diagonal boxes that contained or housed the BBC letter forms. They felt that with the onslaught of satellite TVs the new franchise TV stations coming on board and of course with ITV itself having changed its identity, that it needed to update the whole feel of the organisation, both internally and externally. They came to us and we did with them a lot of research with the public about the BBC and although it is very much a national institution, the feeling was that it was lagging behind in terms of new technology, new programming and the public awareness of the BBC was one that was going backwards and not forwards. We looked at the identity, we started to redesign it, we sharpened up the identity that they already had, but the significant improvement that we did there, was that we made the BBC which is very regional in terms of the BBC in Scotland appeals to the national, to the nation as a group of people. The people want to know what the Scottish local news is all about. Likewise in Wales and likewise in Ireland and England. Therefore we introduced a colour-coded system that would give the consumer a sense of, of it being a local radio and television organisation.

The ATS in fact was a redesign. Again we went through quite a lengthy research programme on that but the interesting thing about that was that Associated Tyre Specialists, which it

was previously called, was quite a mouthful and one of the things that it didn't say was that it didn't talk about the other services that ATS actually offered. People just assumed they offered a service of tyres and not batteries and exhausts and MOTs in fact which was a bulk of the business that ATS actually did. So fundamentally what we did was to abbreviate the name to ATS, make it short and snappy and rather than just change Associated Tyre Specialists and get rid of it, we introduced a set of visual images which visually said or talked about the areas of activity that that company actually did. So we manifested that by a visual image of a battery, a tyre, an exhaust and a symbol for MOTs, which was a spanner, and created something which anybody even devoid of language or awareness of ATS could actually see driving along any High Street.

SPEAKING I

1 Working in pairs, the students are now asked to consider sponsorship as part of a company's corporate identity programme and to think of specific examples. They are most likely to find examples of sports sponsorship, for instance many leading tobacco companies sponsor sports events in an effort to associate their products with a dynamic and healthy outdoor activity.

2 This activity offers students an opportunity to consider the advantages that sponsoring offers a company. In small groups they should read each project and decide which one most appeals to the group. Ensure, where possible, that the individual groups have not all chosen the same project. This can be done by suggesting to undecided groups a project that has not yet been chosen by one of the other groups. All the projects provided could appeal to a computer company looking for an event to sponsor and it is for the students to justify that appeal.

The groups should then consider each of the ten questions provided in the checklist that BC1 would use when deciding which project to sponsor. Go around the different groups checking that this is being done in a systematic way. For example, in relation to the first two questions all the groups will be identifying who BC1's customers are i.e. business people, students in computer studies programmes etc. Groups working on project two will therefore find that they have a strong logical link with the company. However, the other groups will have to develop one. For example, it would be reasonable to assume that the target audience for a chess championship would include the customers of BC1. Likewise it could be interesting for an international computer company to have its name linked with a TV documentary concerning an environmental issue. In this case the students should mention that special care would be taken to show that the company's participation made the filming possible and that they are in no way responsible for the pollution talked about in the programme. The students should be constantly considering what kind of image and/or positive publicity the activity or event could provide for the company. They should be encouraged to take notes about each point they discuss as they will need these to complete the writing task which follows.

WRITING

A model request letter has been provided to help the students complete this task. Check that students respect the layout and that they present their arguments in a clear and persuasive manner.

SPEAKING 2

At this stage of the activity the students are asked to play the role of the directors of a company looking for a project to sponsor. Check that each group reads and considers all the request letters and that they prepare notes for their presentation stage when they will say which project they have chosen and why. The other groups may want to contest the decisions and should be encouraged to give their opinions. During the presentation stage, note down mistakes and following the discussion provide feedback on general or repetitive errors made by the class.